MW00768906

TABLE OF CONTENTS

Acknowledgments

During the course of this project, it was critical to obtain the feedback of many single and divorced people. My questions were often probing and intrusive. I am entirely grateful to have had so many individuals who were willing to grant me an honest, open interview, and to trust me enough with a peek into their private lives. To these people, and to those who participated in the focus groups, I would like to express my sincere gratitude.

I want to also thank my family and closest friends for their support in abiding by my requests to consider my writing life one of complete unavailability for a period of about at least six weeks, during which I completed my work. In particular, I wish to acknowledge the valuable contributions of my friend Lyn Miller, and the enthusiastic unconditional support of my forever friend, Marlene Baggett.

My thanks and appreciation to Andy Terranova, a sponsor of Dale Carnegie Training, for making two very important connections for me: a similarity in my findings with the original principles taught by Mr. Carnegie, and for suggesting that I contact David McDuff of Direct Response Marketing.

Finally, my heartfelt thanks to David McDuff for his insightful contributions and for many spirited discussions, which ultimately served to create a book that was responsive to the needs of its readers. For this, and for the financial support required in bringing this work to publication, I am sincerely grateful. Our meeting was both purposeful and timely. And my thanks to Direct Response Marketing for providing the forum in which we could solicit participants, conduct focus group sessions, and ultimately offer this book.

Introduction

There are numerous books on the subject of dating and relationships. Most of them address what to do and not to do; some provide formulas for long term commitments or marriage. Many of them discuss vehicles for meeting that perfect someone.

This is also a book about dating and will address vehicles for meeting people, but it is not necessarily prescriptive in the sense that it tells you what to do. Rather, it reports pertinent material related to being single and dating and through this material draws some conclusions that may be thought provoking or suggestive. While I identify certain procedures that can be helpful in going about a search, the individual ultimately determines his or her unique strategy for success.

It is easy to appreciate how there may be some fear associated with being 'out there' these days. In an era when prudence is a necessity, growing weary of the dating scene is certainly understandable. Most of us are aware of the constant complaints of unattached people who say things that illustrate their frustration. Still, should we really believe that all the "good ones" are already taken? Can it be that there are no viable methods for meeting people? Is meeting new people all that scary? Of course not, but perceptions are people's reality.

Being single should be a time of introspection and exploration, a time to discover things about ourselves and what we need to be happy. If we aren't having the fun one ought to have while engaged in the quest for a mate, perhaps we need to change the way we are viewing our status and enjoy the moment instead of being too focused on the goal. Thus, with this "labor of love," I hope to make a contribution in helping single people re-establish a fearless approach to dating.

Each of us has acquired a certain amount of information simply from having personally experienced a fair amount of successful and not-so-successful dating. A lifelong student of psychology and human behavior, I have applied my knowledge and experience to what is happening in the current environment. It is the aim of this book to combine this knowledge and experience along with numerous interviews and expert information in creating an informative resource for individuals seeking a satisfying romantic relationship. I hope that those who need to, will hear with a willing mind and an open heart.

In my first book, *There's No Place Like Home*, I discuss the need for us to take responsibility and how we are indeed in control of our own happiness and success. The motivation for that work had to do with the needs I identified while involved in a qualitative research project for a Ph.D. program. It seemed that when people had experienced an involuntary job loss due to a company restructure or shut down, they were left with a sense of despair and feelings of diminished self-worth. This caused them to approach the future with trepidation and circumspection. When I began researching information on singles and dating, it occurred to me that there was a great deal of similarity in how many of the singles approached the prospect of a future relationship. It reminded me of the same willingness to believe that someone else is in control of our happiness and fulfillment in life.

Change is stressful, even if it is good change, and it can wreak havoc in our lives if we allow it. It is always about recognition first and then choosing to respond in a way that brings something positive into our life. In other words, we can choose to be victimized by someone telling us we no longer have our jobs, or when someone with whom we are involved says goodbye, or we can accept it as another experience from which we learn and grow. Allowing it to lower our self-esteem is a choice we have, but it is not the one in our own best interest.

In the course of my investigation, as I looked into the various vehicles for meeting people, it was my good fortune to be introduced to the gentleman responsible for originating the concept of what is now known as "voice personals." This is the evolution of the old newspaper ads where people wrote in to respond to singles in hopes of establishing new friendships and relationships. It worked so well that today over 17 million people use voice personals ads alone, making it clear that the need for people to have options for meeting and dating is being successfully met. The trend is to improve upon the sophistication level of voice personals and other mediums.

After some discussion and negotiation, David W. McDuff decided that he would sponsor this project to offer his clients and potential clients a practical guide to dating. Our meeting was timely. With all the success of the industry he created, he had continued to feel that there was still an unsatisfied need for good advice and had planned to publish such material for some time. This book is the result of our meeting and combination of efforts.

As it turns out, looking for a date is a lot like looking for a job. This is true whether we are brand new at conducting the search or find ourselves unwittingly out there, once again on the "open market," due to some change in our status. We may have been "downsized" or somehow terminated from jobs we thought we would have for a long time. In dating, it's called a breakup of our last relationship, perhaps a marriage. The experiences are similar because they both cause us to go through a certain process of readjustment, evaluation, and finally taking action. Whether we have lost a job or lost a love, there are particular things that will happen and things we will do and will want to do in order to achieve the objective of successful re-attachment.

The analogous descriptions yield applicable techniques for taking action and achieving results. There is, admittedly, a method to meeting people, and there is no intent to deny or discount that here. Methods are procedures for achieving an end, and one good example comes in the form of specific marketing options. This book highlights viable options such as voice personals that many have found to be a terrific source for meeting and dating people.

We usually do not think of how or why we are attracted to certain people until we have experienced failure in our romantic associations. With the majority of us being in that category, possibly even the reason we would even consider reading a book like this, I have attempted to honor that need with a summary of attraction theories. Awareness is always the first step in correction, so I hope you find the explanation that will help you. And since our attractions involve personality, I have included a non-validated version of a questionnaire to assess your behavior style. This assists in the identification of your unique needs and demonstrates how a mate may provide some balance in temperament.

The material then segues into discussions that surfaced from the research, delivering tangible answers to some of the most troubling things about being unattached. Finally, while it does make assertions and suggestions on dating right up to commitment, the reader may be enlightened by what is pertinent and entertained by the rest. Applying the principles known to work in a job search helps us take the kind of action that makes sense for what we want in a love relationship. Using specific feedback obtained from actual interviews, questionnaires, and focus group sessions allows me to provide realistic, comprehensive advice.

What none of the dating books can help with, and this book is no exception, is the responsibility we have to ourselves to live a meaningful life. Life's fulfillment is often measured by the relationships we build with people we choose to have in our lives. Our love life should meet our needs, but not before we have met our own. We are probably best advised not to enter into a love relationship with another until we have had one with ourselves. This is a crucial distinction, and until we learn it, we will continue to be presented with numerous opportunities for lessons in the form of potential life partners. Happiness will never depend upon the presence or absence of someone in our life; it will depend only on the quality of our choices as we respond to what happens.

So, here's to all the Single People of the World: May you find Peace with your Status, And One day, *love yourself into* a relationship…

♥ ♥ ♥

One

OUR STORY

A part of us keeps thinking that our worth as a human being will be determined by the desirability of the mate we are able to attract. ...(We) look for a person who throws (us) into a trance, and hope that when (we) come out of the trance, he turns out to be someone (we) can like.

Harold S. Kushner
How Good Do We Have To Be? 1996, (pp. 100, 102)

From the time we begin thinking of romance, we start to form tiny descriptive pictures in our head. Like pieces to a puzzle, we continue to add to this picture, ultimately resulting in a complete sketch including everything from what our perfect person looks like, to their occupation, the kind of car they drive, even what activities we will enjoy together.

By the time we are in our twenties, this picture comes into relatively good focus. We think we know what we want and need. We must have this; we will not take that. We are selective and we should be. Partnership and commitment are not necessarily predominant in our minds, however. We have other things with which we are concerned, like career, travel, and mostly just hanging out with friends. After all, we will never be this free again, once we settle down and take on the serious responsibilities of a monogamous relationship and starting a family.

By our late twenties, if we remain unmarried until then, our sketch has been modified. That's understandable, as we have usually had many dates by then and have learned a thing or two ... even if it is what we absolutely do NOT want. Given a choice between who some of our friends marry and nothing, we'd rather remain single. Generally, we still expect that what happened to them will never happen to us, and so we remain open and optimistic.

Our thirties arrive too soon and even in these modern times, concern gradually escalates. We wouldn't ever get so anxious if we were left alone, but here comes Mom with her cautionary reminders about how we're not getting any younger. And Aunt Mary and Cousin Sue and dear ole' Grandma warning us about 'being alone'… "You don't want to, *do you*?" Time is passing you by, your friends are passing you by, my God, life is passing you by! And so sets the stage for the not-so-flirty thirties.

We have all kinds of thoughts about those who have never been married by the time they reach their forties or fifties. Are these "confirmed bachelors and bachelorettes?" Are they gay? Perhaps they are anti-social, selfish, somehow "weird." No one would ever *choose* to be single, would they??? No, something *must* be wrong…. We wonder about them, perhaps even pity and avoid them. They may pose a threat, or their lives may be enviable. Amid the conjectures, these singles are not only aware of what's being said-- some hurt by it, others unaffected—but they know that they will inevitably reach the age when they are referred to as simply "never marries."

Men and women everywhere are flustered. It was fun being single in our late teens, early twenties. But once the thirties descend upon us, something changes. A lot does, actually. Friends we used to party with have gone the way of the committed life. While at first we laugh at them, we now consider that *they* could actually be having the better time. The joke may be on us after all. We vacillate, have moments of second-guessing; is this mere reaction? Are we going through a temporary "life looks a little greener on the other side" perception? Someone warned us about these things ... it only *looks* that way from where we're standing.

Eventually our original picture of the 'perfect' someone takes on variations and further modifications. We go from the guy with the ideal profession to the one with a decent career...then, to just *having a job*. That's it! All we want is for him to be *employed* ... Or for her to be *"half-way* decent looking." So now we are clear that he no longer has to make a lot of money and she no longer has to be a size 5 beauty queen. Anyway, we rationalize, "those people" are full of themselves. They have their own problems. It's best this way. And so instead of Mr./Ms. Right, we *settle* for Mr./Ms." ALLright."

The problem with this thought pattern is that it is too externally focused. Everything seems to be about the other person...that "special someone." We figure that "*the*" one particular someone must have been taken; we were too slow, not at the right place, let alone the right time. Maybe our perfect person was hung up somewhere, unable to get to us, probably was at that party we were supposed to go to. What rotten luck! I missed him, she missed me, they missed out. When we focus outward, expecting someone to be our answer to happiness, we are bound to feel disappointed and victimized.

Some of us may even do the marriage thing with our Mr./Ms. ALLright, keeping a furtive eye out for Mr./Ms. Perfect, who we still believe is out there. One might think of it as a rather practical approach, actually: *I'll just do this okay thing, but should the perfect person arrive, well, divorce IS an option...* a rather easily available one at that, these days.

Naturally, women have a much worse case of the time factor than do their male counterparts. They have the proverbial "biological clock" ticking away. Sometimes it gets so loud, they'll do almost anything to silence the noise ... even marry the first guy who *asks* -- or scare away the ones who don't ask quite fast enough!

But there are obviously a number of unattached males who have also expressed the desire to at least be involved in a long-term relationship. They may not be quick to call what they seek anything permanent like a *marriage*, but they express a similar sense of weariness after numerous unsuccessful dates and relationships. The truth is that in the end, men and women are often quite similar in their desire for a committed relationship in which they are able to experience mutually satisfying unconditional love and acceptance.

Unfortunately, it doesn't always look that way. Women and men often feel misunderstood by one another. One might be playing a game in which the other doesn't know the rules, may not even wish to play. We're reading between lines and interpreting indirect language, which often makes any game a guessing one at best. Through it all, it can be a challenge to get the man and woman ready for a "serious relationship" at the same time. The problem will always be that where communication leaves off, imagination takes over, and our imaginations are usually far worse than reality.

When it comes to communication and interpretation, the experts tell us that men and women are very different. We are told that women speak a different language than men. Differing genetic endowments and socialization aspects notwithstanding, we now hear how we may have originated from separate planets! We must learn how we can be sensitive to these major differences, mastering the language that allows us to talk to one another without offense.

The newly single, or once-again single have little advantage when it comes to dating and finding a new mate. In fact, they may be at some disadvantage depending on their age, the nature of their breakup, and the availability of their network. If they hadn't been "prepared," with a couple of prospects out in the wings, they can feel disenfranchised. And if children happen to be involved, it's a whole other ballgame.

With at least a 50 percent divorce rate in the United States, we know that we are doing something wrong. It wouldn't be alarming if there weren't children to be concerned with, but in so many of the cases, we do have families. The pain involved in these breakups extends beyond the individual couple and often spills over into subsequent love relationships.

Consequently, a growing number of single parents are added to the number of dating prospects with ages ranging from their 20s to 60s. Then we have the people still actively looking who may have lost a spouse through death, and this age group can take us in to the 80s. So that we have a whole gamut of single prospects who may have even greater fear about dating than those who have never married. They do not want to repeat their mistakes and they aren't always sure how to do that. They may throw themselves in the ring prematurely in reaction to a breakup, only to end up in another bad relationship. They may spend an inordinate amount of time held back in suspicion of others and anger at what happened, hindering their own peace of mind and happiness. Or they may remain in a bitter, resentful, depressive state, withdrawing the idea of ever loving again, remaining alone and lonely.

Whether we have failed at a relationship once, twice, or more, all it says about us is that we may be thinking wrongly. The way we think determines how we ultimately behave because our actions are the ultimate manifestations of our beliefs about who we are. If we believe that our happiness is up to someone in our lives, then we place responsibility for our happiness in the hands of someone over whom we have no control. Yet, if we say and believe that our happiness is our gift to ourselves, then we empower ourselves, knowing that we are indeed in control. So when someone leaves us or treats us badly, we have a choice to respond in a way that takes care of ourselves and allows us to feel good about ourselves, no matter what the other person does. Not only would we not want that person in our lives because they do not meet with our dominant thoughts about how we deserve to be treated, but also their absence has nothing to do with our happiness. When self-love and self-respect motivates our thinking, we act in accordance with that premise, making it unlikely that we end up in situations that fail to support those positive beliefs.

"Our story," as I have named it, is the story with which we have the greatest familiarity, but that is only because we have made it so. We can change it any day we decide it is time for a change. It won't matter if we are just starting to date and never been married, or if we are on our second or third marriage. While we won't be able to control all of life's circumstances, we will always be able to choose our response to what happens. Our response will dictate the level of happiness and satisfaction we feel in our lives, so why not choose to preserve that happiness?

If we can only remember that our source of strength is nowhere outside us, with no one outside ourselves, we would be less affected by societal dictates and more led by what is in our hearts. There we will find no time by which we need to marry, no standards that we need to meet to find ourselves worthy of someone, and no erroneous beliefs in a one perfect person theory.

When we are happy, we act happy, and draw positive people to our lives who simply enhance our existing state of happiness. In other words, our "perfect mate" arrives naturally once we assume responsibility and have no onerous expectations of them. We won't expect them to make us happy, we will simply invite them to join us in our happiness.

♥ ♥ ♥

DateNotes

- If you are just beginning, perhaps in your twenties, know that this is a great time for figuring out who you are and what you want.

- Try not to allow any external pressure to dictate your next step because of what others are doing at a similar age. Accept your uniqueness as perfect as it is for you and trust your intuition.

- Thirty is a great age to enter into a serious relationship or even marriage, but if you haven't yet, know that this is somehow purposeful for you. Perhaps there is something you need to do first…or *instead.*

- Whatever you do, do not settle. It is particularly sad to learn how many of us were actually consciously aware that *something was wrong* when we entered into a legally binding relationship. Always "listen" to your feelings, as they are the windows to your heart and soul.

- When we settle, we set ourselves up to fail. Not only will we experience inevitable unhappiness and regret, but the day will arrive when someone will make perfect sense, but we won't be free to pursue that relationship. Whether or not you actually get to meet this person, know that *it could have been* right for you.

- Please trust that where you are is where you need to be and that if and when you are ready, the "right" relationship will find you. Readiness does include availability, of course, but it is also about having completed your personal work first.

- Even as that is said, this does not mean that you should do nothing and sit home every night waiting for your prince or princess to join you. What it does say is that you need to relax and believe that it will happen when it is right for you. In the meantime, have fun dating and meeting lots of interesting people.

- If you are one of the forty and fifty-somethings who find them selves newly single after a failed marriage, understand that the lessons you have learned were essential for your progress. You will repeat them if you have not learned what they were to teach you.

- Remember that happiness is not circumstance dependent, so it isn't about who you are with that makes you happy. Our happiness is our own responsibility and we will always have all we need to experience a satisfying life.

- Since happiness is a choice we make, why not choose to be happy just the way it is right now? Can you imagine how appealing and attractive that might be to someone looking at you?

Two

APPLYING THE PRINCIPLES OF AN EFFECTIVE SEARCH:

Stage 1: "Reality Check"

When one door closes, another opens. But we often look so long and so regretfully at the closed door that we do not notice the one which has opened for us.

Alexander Graham Bell

Whether we are brand new at job seeking or find ourselves back in the market after a disappointing job loss, we are assaulted by the enormity of the task. We cannot believe that we have to work so hard, be so organized, and see so many people. Defining our objectives, networking and marketing ourselves, all to get to the interview for decision-making takes time and energy. Perhaps we should try to have a little fun, as long as we are engaged in the process. If it's the first time around, that's one thing. But if we have been in one place for awhile, we are finding ourselves brushing up on things that we hadn't had to think about in what seems like forever.

It's the same in dating. Once we have made the decision to begin the search process, we need to establish what we are looking for and take advantage of ways to market ourselves. Our objective will be to screen and interview as many potential candidates as possible before making a decision, which can take a fair amount of energy. And, we understand that the decision needs to be a mutual one: both parties must be happy with the match.

In the aftermath of a life-altering event, we always have one of two choices: We can either react or respond. Reactions are never positive, as they are motivated by fear and cause us to engage in defensive behaviors. We can't learn when we are busy being defensive, and we cannot move, either. It is best to respond. This means that we are thinking clearly to develop a plan for solving our problem and getting what we want in the end. Our motivation is focused on this desire and so it remains positive. This is the difference between being paralyzed by the problem or perceiving the opportunity in the change.

For our purposes here, we will assume that the reader has had at least one previous experience, from which they likely emerge somewhat wounded. Some of us are more seriously injured by the experience, and others of us can pick ourselves up again with relative ease. Still, we may not only need a reality check, we may require some emotional assistance to mobilize us in discovering what may be the best thing that's ever happened to us. Reacting to a job loss often means anger and a fractured self-esteem. In a reaction mode following a romantic breakup, we are often blinded by negative emotion. While our responsiveness may entail a sadness, we will move through the loss with open eyes and willing hearts.

When we become upset over the absence or loss of love in our life, we go through a "grieving process," similar to those who have lost a job. We had something, it didn't work out, now we need to move on with grace and dignity. The only problem is that we want to ensure that we have learned from the previous experience and we have benefited from the lessons we have learned. We need a strategy to help us. But, we're not there yet.

First, we are shocked by the loss and we hope it really isn't true. It's a bad dream from which we shall awake soon enough. This is called denial and it is a stage during which we may not be ready to be with anyone or do anything yet. Then, we become angry. Just as the guy who lost the job wants someone to blame, our inclination after a breakup might be to lay blame at the feet of anyone or anything we can conjure up. If we have trouble integrating the change, we might even condemn the statistics, criticizing the "leftovers." All the good ones are already married! Getting angry is okay, as it is a natural and healthy part of the process, so long as we do not become bitter. If we have made progress out of the anger stage, we may try to postpone the inevitable by attempting to bargain our way out of it. We try to convince ourselves that if we only do this or say that, we could save ourselves from this fate. This is usually a mental exercise, but it can manifest in ways where it impairs the person's ability to move on and accept responsibility. In depression, we experience lowered energy and self-esteem, but in some way may be on our way to resolution of our problem. Still, for the moment we have turned on ourselves, as depression is anger turned inward: *What do I do so wrong in meeting people and getting them to love me!?*

Keeping busy may assist us while in a depressed state, and when we are ready, we can see our way to accepting what has happened. A support system of people who care also helps in reassuring us and in lending a listening ear. Perhaps we have learned a good deal from the experience, and can now design a plan of action to achieve something new and better for ourselves. With a job loss, it may be that we were misplaced anyway, needed a kick to get us thinking about what it is we really want and need to be happy. If it is a severed relationship, we likely have much to learn from it as well, especially about ourselves. In both, it will take courage to get back in and move forward with our lives.

There is another parallel to be drawn between the loss of a job and the loss of a romantic partner and this concerns the element of time. People who have invested years into a particular career, usually in a particular company, generally operate under an assumption that they have "paid their dues" and can relax a bit. They have given of themselves, and have made some plans contingent on that part of their lives remaining constant. Often these people are in their 40s, and on some level acknowledge that they are on the back side of their careers. When these people are jolted by the reality that they are being terminated, it often turns their world upside down. They are unsure of their futures. They didn't think they would have to be confronted with updating their resume, maintaining an active schedule of networking and interviewing with people, much less the loss of a reliable source of income and established coworker relationships. The relationships with people at work became important as they often spent more time with coworkers than they did their own families. Just when they thought they could relax, all hell broke lose, sometimes shattering their confidence, beliefs, and trust.

Talk to anyone who has invested a number of years in a long-time relationship only to have it end, and it often sounds very similar. These are the people who felt that they had given what they should and could and really believed that the payback for that time and loyalty and support would be there. Now, they aren't so sure what their futures will be. Just when they thought they didn't need to worry so much about looking great or fighting so hard to climb that corporate ladder, someone comes along and shatters their beliefs. They find themselves back out there, needing to be concerned about their appearance, having to figure out how to meet other available people, and not particularly enthusiastic about "dating." All the while, they secretly hope that other available people aren't all losers and aren't thinking of them in the same way.

The one thing that continues to surprise me, however, is not so much the reactions of these individuals. The fact that they are upset, angry, caustic, sometimes jaded from a dramatic life experience is understandable. But when we ask these same folks, "well, *were* you happy?" they have great difficulty responding with an unequivocal yes. I find that entirely interesting and curious, a phenomenon that I believe is so worthy of study.

I did study the behavior of middle-aged professionals following an involuntary loss of a job in which they had invested a number of years. In the course of the investigation, it occurred to me that we had identified certain guiding questions such as how they felt upon learning the news, why did they feel this way, and how have their attitudes and beliefs been affected as they go forward?

I thought I would get answers that would explain why some people bounced back so easily after such an experience, while others appeared to be more devastated and therefore lacking in motivation to become re-employed. What I found was that while some were more upset than others, I was gleaning more information about who these people were and how that correlated with their responses or reactions. I began to revise my questioning to reflect the discovery that included why these people had lost their jobs. Had they done something? Were they just unlucky, or doomed to fail due to some predisposition in their thought system? In other words, would these people be here if they had thought differently? Did they lose their jobs because the original fit was a bad one? And if so, what led them to their choice in the first place?

Luck is always an untenable aspect. I dismissed it with relative ease. And, as far as all my investigation would lead me, these people had done nothing "wrong." In fact, by most standards, these were employees who had been valued and highly skilled professionals.

That's when I began to ask about happiness. I found I could ask a lot of questions. I asked whether they were happy with the original choice they had made, and if not, why didn't they do something about it earlier. I asked about passionate work, their thoughts and beliefs about it, and if they ever felt a passion toward their work.

When I speak to individuals who are experiencing or have experienced the end of a long-term love relationship, I have the same thoughts about the notion of "luck" and of having "done something wrong." Most of us realize that no one leaves us and we don't leave them because of something one of us has done wrong. Unless the act is catastrophic or repeated, we are humans and accept one another for our imperfect behavior. Inevitably, however, what I find, whether it is the individual who leaves or the one who is left, is a person who *was not happy*.

Now, did they know they were unhappy? It seems funny to ask the question in this way, but I really am not convinced of the consciousness with which people live their lives. Therefore, we are in jobs and in marriages, not necessarily because we are happy, but because of other things like complacency, family ties, and just unsure of what happiness really is, or if it's even attainable.

When I inquired about passionate work, my participants seemed to believe that only certain persons get to reflect that level in their work life. One even mentioned Vincent Van Gogh as an example. For the most part, these people defined a job as a job. They hadn't thought of work necessarily as something we should love to do. But they did feel betrayed, mostly because they were good people doing good jobs and expected that to be rewarded. This all got me questioning how we go about deciding what career we will pursue, and now, how we decide with whom to have a long-term relationship.

Here are my final questions:

• Are we conscious about our happiness?

• Are we where we are and with whom we are because of love, or something *other* than really wanting to be there?

• What are the criteria we use when we are selecting a career or a mate? Are we not passionate about the work or the mate we have chosen? Do we feel that this achievement is an ideal, reserved for only a "lucky few?"

• Do we end up losing in the end because we were a poor fit to begin with? And if so, is this a real loss, and how can we be sure that it won't happen again?

As I had concluded in my original study, I have to believe prevention is far better than having to come up with the cure, if prevention is feasible. By that I mean if nothing else, if we can do nothing about having lost a job or a mate we thought we would have for the duration, we *can* change how we view what we deserve out of life. That way, there is a greater likelihood that we won't repeat a choice that will result in the same sense of despair we experienced the first (or last) time around.

Also, if and when we do have children, we will have done them the greatest favor of all. They will learn from us, as they always do, what love is and what they deserve. They will choose both what they do for a living and with whom they have relationships from an emotionally healthy point of view. The one which reinforces their high levels of self-worth.

Ultimately, we need to feel a sense of control of our lives and not look for happiness in some company, spouse, or circumstance. A sense of control can be achieved through the acknowledgment of choice, particularly during bad times. Viktor Frankl developed Logotherapy which addresses the concept of suffering (Brammer, 1991). He explains:

> *Suffering is a subjective experience as well as a reaction to an objective event. It is not only the way things are that leads to suffering; it is sometimes our reactions to those events. ...Although we cannot always change the tragic circumstances of our lives, we can choose how we are going to react to those events* (Brammer, 1991, p.37).

Author Daniel Goleman, Ph.D., who wrote *Emotional Intelligence*

(1995) explains how optimists view failure as changeable, while pessimists take blame and feel helpless to change. When people feel there is something they can do in a negative situation, some control they can exert, they fare better emotionally than those who feel helpless. Goleman feels that self-control and the ability to motivate oneself are among the characteristics included in possessing emotional intelligence and that these *can* be taught. Accepting his thoughts on instilling optimism and self-motivation makes sense, but providing people with the tools necessary to feel a sense of personal control seems a moral imperative. In adult life, this is at least partly achieved through developing a competency, but there is the other consideration for the guidance of our young people. In an effort toward prevention, we properly guide them, nurture them, and assure them that they are whole, worthwhile human beings who are entirely capable of creating their own futures to be all that they wish themselves to be.

Stage 2: Assessment

The unexamined life is not worth living.

Socrates

The first thing that counselors inform job seekers is to take stock of what they have to offer. This is important, as it helps in some measure with maintaining a positive self-esteem, and ensures that they are conscious of their worth to prospective employers.

It's really a lot like seeking a mate. The mental preparation prior to getting up the nerve to approach someone has to involve some element of knowing who we are, what we want, and what kinds of partnerships are most suited to our needs.

So we say, know what you are interested in and what you are not. We are naturally attracted to people with similar interests; it makes life easier that way. Know too, who you are, what you value, and how another person might fit in with that picture. Remember, you have come with a learned set of experiences; you have matured and are ready to do it better this time. Having a conscious awareness of your needs along with the benefit of experience ensures that you have far greater preparation, and therefore potential for success, than the last time around.

Going forward without this kind of self-assessment may be a mistake. This is why employment counselors warn candidates not to jump right back in and become re-employed immediately, if they can help it. It is a time for taking one step back before taking the step forward. Otherwise, it's possible that we will proceed with a less-than-conscious approach to finding a suitable work life or love life. Think about what happened the first or last time. Was it conscious then? Did we just "fall into the position," or "end up dating" and then just married, because it was the right thing to do, the right time, or the person everyone thought we *should* marry? Many of us conduct our lives with this kind of unconscious behavior that gets us in trouble and causes us to repress the notion of true happiness. And when action precedes thought out of ignorance or desperation, it is easy to forget who we are or what we need.

I used to think that most people lacked this sense of consciousness when they selected careers and jobs, but I am afraid that there is a similar attitude in selecting a mate. We know this because statistics reveal our failure rates, and remember, in marriage alone we are wrong at least fifty percent of the time. This book is intended to raise our consciousness, to cause us to consider who we are and what we need prior to making a decision to date someone. And while we can have real fun in the process of that selection, we want to think it through before entering into a serious relationship or commitment.

Ideally, we wouldn't move forward with a new life plan before getting over the old, either. That would not be fair to someone we are dating, and it is not even fair to ourselves. We need to promise that we won't do this; that at least we will be better for the lessons we have learned, from the education we will have received. The reason all this bears mention is because once we have progressed to the stage where we are considering how we will search for a mate, residual feelings for an old one will surely sabotage the new.

That from which we emerge uneducated is that which we are bound to repeat. It is said that the definition of insanity is doing the same thing over and over and expecting different results. Don't be insane.

Over the many years that I have been addressing large groups of people, it never ceases to amaze me how little time we actually grant ourselves in the self-assessment process. We have busy lives, we have things we do, and things we've got to get done. We have families that demand our attention and friends for whom we try desperately to make time. Time for ourselves may resemble a quick work out or squeezing in some moments before bedtime to catch up on some much-desired reading. When someone like me comes along to question who we are and why we do what we do, we either laugh, because we can't believe how silly this line of questioning feels, or cry because we regret our circumstances. We know intellectually that we make time for what we deem important, so does this really mean that we hold time for ourselves in such very low regard? How do we create happy lives with successful relationships when we don't even begin to understand who we are and what we need? We are too busy doing and not busy enough just *being*, which is the only way that we can hear our hearts speak to us.

People inevitably say that they were never trained to assess themselves, to listen to their hearts and determine what they need. And it's true, most of us were not likely taught that there is validity in trusting our instincts, that we ought to have confidence in our sense of purpose, whatever that happens to be. Instead, we are pushed and shoved in to spaces and places, and before you know it we are pushing and shoving ourselves when we don't even know why. How do we question this when it is all that we have known? We haven't said, *stop the world, I wanna get off*, we can only think and do what's on automatic pilot because we don't know any better. What happens is that we usually find ourselves in midlife faced with the clarity of our mortality and wondering what this whole life thing is about.

The best news that we can have and understand and believe is that today is a new day. We can do today what we wish we had done yesterday, not blaming one single soul, only taking responsibility for our own futures, right now.

Stage 3 Marketing Options

Smart women understand that meeting a man does not involve simply being in the "right place at the right time." It requires creating those situations. These women assume an active role in designing their lives in such a way as to enhance their chances of coming in contact with interesting men.

Smart Women, Foolish Choices (1985), Dr. Connell Cowan and Dr. Melvyn Kinder

[Note: Although this quote directed itself to women, it seems obvious that it can apply to men about women, as well.]

This is where the fun enters in. Once we have decided to move forward with our search, we have a number of options available to us. In designing our marketing plan, we might list those available options, and weigh their value to us at this particular time:

We can go through agents. These are people who will market us to prospective matches. In the dating world, this can mean anything from a computer dating service to our friends and relatives who wish to set us up with someone they know. Some people consider this one of the most desirable and convenient ways to meet others, even as we recognize that it can be potentially stressful. Although there is an introduction by and through a mutual friend or acquaintance, it is still similar to a "blind date." Utilizing such agents does present a way that we can reasonably come in to contact with people like us, looking to spend time and perhaps end up with a new friend, if nothing more. Still, whether for the purposes of a job search or mate search, we must be careful not to completely rely on someone else to do our job. If we fail to convey our interests and concerns in a clear and honest manner, it can lead to negative consequences.

In most computer dating services, the sign-up is generally followed by an interview designed to obtain information about who we are and what we are looking for, and to match that criteria with another individual's profile in their database. We are usually handed a certain number of matches for a particular price. There may even be an opportunity for us to attend a videotaped viewing of the individual selected. There is a concern that many people are reluctant to sit before a video camera and speak about themselves. And if this is true, we may be limiting ourselves to a smaller audience than other options afford. As with all other vehicles, sometimes this works and other times it does not. If we sign on with such a service, we ought to be willing to give it enough time before deciding one way or the other.

Personal agents will always have the best intentions as they are people who love us, care about us, and believe that they understand what we are looking for. They have observed us, and are often sure that they know what we need. When they are wrong, however (and sometimes they can be dreadfully wrong), we risk hurting their feelings and possibly jeopardizing our relationship with them. Someone may know us as a sibling or as a friend, but they don't know what it is like to date us and may even lack objectivity when "selling us."

I spoke to one woman who told me a story about a man she had met through her well-meaning brother. She was 36, once divorced, no children, and he was 40, never married. She recalled him telling her how she needn't worry because he comes with no "baggage," referring to ex-wives and children. As she recounted the story, she sarcastically added that he may not have had any 'physical' baggage, but he certainly had a barrelfull of emotional stuff he was carrying around. When I questioned why she had dated him for nearly two years she said, "I needed to give it enough time because of my brother." She was sure that probably most people in her situation would've done the same. Feelings of obligation may keep us in there much longer than we would otherwise choose to be.

Another story involved a 37-year-old gentleman who complained that his married friends were so concerned about him that they were constantly arranging for him to meet available women. Since one friend's wife was a social worker, she regularly came in contact with a number of single mothers who needed assistance. At first he obliged them by attending each of the dinners set up at their home to meet another woman, but soon he declined. He believed that although these friends really meant well, they probably were not terribly discriminating, thinking that just about any woman might be interesting to meet and possibly be "the one."

Single people over age 30 find that things change for them once most of their friends have married. First of all, the network that had once worked well in their twenties is now comprised of people who are couples, some of whom are starting families and no longer going out regularly. These couples also know fewer and fewer singles. What those beyond 30 may also encounter are people that have already been married once, some having had children. This becomes increasingly a consideration the older one becomes.

The Internet continues to gain popularity among individuals looking to market job skills or meet someone, and systems advancements to facilitate that process are being made daily. The advantage of using the Internet to meet new people is that we can literally explore the globe from our home or office. Interested individuals may wish to check out two sites,www.DATE-FINDER.com. and www.PLANETULTIMATE.com.

Members pay a small monthly fee to belong. They give detailed information about themselves that can be used as search criteria to find others. Members can see video's of each other with voice greetings and can enter chat rooms or purchase products such as flowers, books, and dating-related items. As with voice personals, the Internet "surfer" can remain anonymous until the time they feel adequately comfortable in revealing their identity.

Internet users are generally different demographically from newspaper voice personals' users. They are typically younger, more computer literate, and in general more receptive to a long distance relationship. There may be a good deal more in the way of preliminary communication prior to a face-to-face meeting, but this might be a good thing. We can learn a lot about someone through the written word and lengthy telephone conversations.

When dating using the personals ads first began, it was necessary to write letters in response to the ads. Since the written word was all the two individuals knew about one another, it was important to do a good job in highlighting who we were and what we had to offer a prospective date. Today, considerable improvements have been made to facilitate the process, eliminating the need to spend long hours responding by mail and leaving more time for us to explore. This updated, more sophisticated version of personals ads dating is what is known today as "voice personals."

If we choose to use voice personals, we can be the one who places the ad, usually for free. It costs nothing to dial in to the 800 number, which initiates contact with a computerized voice system that asks us a series of questions, or we may speak to a live operator. We can attempt to attract an interested date just by the choice of words we use in responding to the questions. The most that is required is that we take the time and thought to succinctly express who we are in order to elicit the kind of responses from the type of people we would indeed be interested in meeting.

Placing the Ad:
The "Summary Statement"

The voice personals ad itself would be considered the summary statement in a well-written resume. The idea is for the ad to briefly state what the individual has to say about themselves and at the same time what they may be looking for in a mate. We tell job seekers that it is often only the brief summary statement that is read before an employer decides to speak with the individual. This is because most of the time they do not want to read much more before they make a quick determination on whether the candidate sounds like someone worthy of a face-to-face meeting. Even though it is a mere summary, however, we can see why it is important that it says what needs to be said in as few words possible.

The summary statement, or ad, gets the ball rolling. The objective is the interview, after all. All that happens in the preliminary stage is to gain the appropriate attention, motivate ongoing interest, and sustain the attraction. Once that is accomplished, we look forward to the moment when we can sit across from one another in person, and figure out whether it makes sense to fish or cut bait.

The Mechanics:
How it works

Voice personals have other advantages besides being free to the one who places the ad. It is an efficient, expedient way for many individuals (on both sides of it) who are too busy to pursue someone in other ways. It exposes one seeking dates to the greatest possible audience in a concentrated period of time. It allows the one who has placed the ad to talk to as many people as they like, and after some telephone screening activity, to meet as many as they perhaps can and want to. This grants the advertiser total control over the process, allowing them to manage their own search campaign the way they want to, at their own pace.

There are two facets to the telephone contact. The initial stage is when the respondent calls to leave a message on the advertiser's "voice mailbox." As the respondent, it is probably a good idea to let the person know why they captured our interest. There is a fee for leaving the message, generally from $1.99-$2.49 per minute, so we need to be mindful about a few things:

- What we say
- How we say it
- How we address the reason for our interest, and
- Why we believe the individual should call us.

Remember, we have no benefit of visual cues when we leave a message, so it is important that we take the time to consider what we would like to convey.

The other facet involves the return call from the one who placed the ad. Obviously, if they have determined from the respondent's message that he or she is someone they wish to speak to, they will call. If they have decided that this is an unlikely match, then the call will probably not be returned.

In cases where there is a call back, we assume that the message stirred interest and somehow motivated the advertiser to at least talk with this individual. If after the "screening" return phone call there is no further interest, then neither party has risked anything, as it is unlikely they exchanged specific, private information. Nothing is lost but a few moments of time-- time not wasted since the discovery took place early on and both identities may remain anonymous. It is entirely to our benefit, on either side of the call, to conduct a thorough telephone-screening job before agreeing to meet someone face-to-face.

In summation, here are two points worth mention. The first is that there is an obvious responsibility for the individual placing the ad to think through what they wish to say in order to represent themselves accurately. As one woman said to me, "You shouldn't advertise for apples if you want oranges." There is also a responsibility for the respondent to leave an adequate voice message to get the individual to want to speak further with them. Second, in order to maintain privacy and safety, the conversation ought to be about determining similar interests without revealing too much personal detail during the initial telephone callback. If there is interest, we could agree to meet in a public place where we can maintain our own personal safety.

Speaking about safety, the industry has gone to great lengths to ensure the confidentiality of its clients in recent years. For example, many voice personal services offer a "confidential mail box option," which allows a respondent to have a place where the advertiser can call and respond to their message. They never have to disclose their phone number. So if a woman is interested in contacting a gentleman whose ad appears in the newspaper, she can call in to the mailbox and reveal her interest, saying that she would prefer to call him. Then, the choice is his to leave his number for contact to be made. Caution is always prudent when engaging in what may prove to be a rather active schedule of meeting new people.

Voice personals will provide what they call "computer matches," based on certain set criteria. But there is no obligation for the user to call these people. Each step of the way we are able to maintain control, no matter how many people we decide to talk to and ultimately meet.

There are obviously individuals who only respond to ads, and that's fine, too. Again, however, like the job seeker, we place ourselves in the hopeful position of getting called when there are potentially a large number of respondents, who may be just as "qualified" as we are.

The best way to diminish the concern of being one of numerous respondents to a personal ad is to choose to place one. We can still respond to other ads, but have one of our own, to which others can respond. In this way, we are not reduced to merely hoping that we will be the one to get selected, to get a return call. We effectively increase the level of control we have over our own situation as others will respond to our ad and the choice is ours on who to call back.

Obviously, not everyone who calls someone in response to an ad can receive a return call. We need not take it too personally. Why would we want someone to call us who isn't interested, anyway? It could be that our telephone message is inadequate or unappealing and failed to attract the interest we would have liked. It also could mean that the individual was inundated with calls, making such ultimate courtesies unrealistic and impractical. Still, as respondent we have one of three choices:

One, we could call a second time, and leave another message. It could be one that is totally creative or silly, in any case, attention getting, this time. Of course, we could find other ads that interest us. Or, we could place an ad ourselves, and be in the driver's seat.

Here are some tips when using the Voice Personals service to meet and date other people who are probably very much like you:

• The message you leave someone is very important. Try writing out your voice message before you record it. Be informative and creative and avoid using unclear language that could be interpreted in various ways. When you leave a message, stand out from the many others by referring to your interests and desires, while somehow addressing theirs (from their ad) specifically.

• If you are the one who placed the ad, you have just established a rejection-proof dating vehicle for yourself. You've already done the asking, by placing the ad, and you'll never have to be hurt by those who choose not to respond to you, because you will never even have to know who they are. On the other hand, you will hear from only those who are interested in meeting you and you get to select them, based on your level of interest after conversing with them.

On the responding side, you should not take a lack of call back as a rejection, either. First of all, you don't really know who the person is, and they don't know who you are, so how could you feel rejected? Just try calling someone else who sounds interesting. There are plenty to choose from.

• Charm and sex appeal come from being your *real* self. Be honest. Remember that if you end up meeting the person, it won't be so comfortable if you've been less than accurate in your previous conversations with them. Try not to play games. You want the person to like *you*, not someone you may pretend to be. If they like the person you made up, you're not going to feel any better about yourself, and you'll surely jeopardize any potential for a successful relationship.

• An initial telephone contact may be like asking for a person's resume. You will want to conduct a somewhat thorough screening job before you agree to meet the individual face to face. Be prepared with your questions; the answers will get you the information you need to make a proper evaluation and decision. Remember, you are using a medium to meet people that affords you a tremendous advantage: To speak to a large number of prospective dates, prior to deciding that you are interested. Use it wisely. Get to know someone over the phone before meeting him or her face-to-face.

• Be confident. You have nothing to lose when your first contact is by telephone. The best that can happen is that you have an interesting conversation, possibly meet an interesting person, or even a new friend. The worst that can happen is that you lose a little of your time during the screening interview process.

Be respectful of the other person's privacy by not expecting or demanding too much of them or the potential relationship. Be patient, too. Getting to know someone takes time.

• If you do agree to meet someone, you are essentially going on a blind date. When you arrive, be careful not to judge the person on looks alone by turning around and walking away. The courteous and courageous thing to do is to sit down and have a face-to-face conversation. Chances are that if you liked them enough over the phone to meet them, you owe it to yourself-*and them*- to discover more and see it through at least to this first meeting.

• We should know that dates are to be enjoyed, relationships are created, and love is developed. You may as well have as much fun as you like by dating as many people as you want to before you're ready for the more serious affair of a long-lasting love relationship. Look at it this way: the more we have to choose from, the greater the likelihood we'll find the best match possible.

• When you're finally on the date, don't begin to worry immediately about where it's going—that's sure to ruin the fun of the moment. Maintain an attitude of open-mindedness –which may lead you to pleasant surprises.

• Why not shop around by using the browse option in voice personals, which invites you to broaden your search by using more flexible criteria. It's designed for people who aren't all that certain of what they want or need in a partner, or for individuals who wish to remain open about the possibilities. Who knows? Lots of people report having a great time just exploring and meeting people they'd otherwise not have the opportunity to meet!

• Think positively and do expect the best to happen. While not every one you speak to will be someone you'd like to date or expect to get serious with, in the short-term, we can find good conversation and friendships-- even if we don't develop relationships for awhile. Enjoy the adventure!

One final point. Just as in a job search, learning the art of "networking" is probably a very good idea. When we open ourselves up to the possibilities, we meet new people who know other people. Be receptive to all the possible connections that can be made.

Taking the Opportunity Approach to Meeting People

This is an interesting dilemma to single people today, particularly in an era of AIDS and the verbal disillusionment of the bar scene (I say it this way because for as many people who complain about them, large numbers continue to frequent the bars--perhaps it is mostly twenty-somethings). What happens is that the so called "bar scene" gets old real quick, and we get old too quick, so there is little surprise so many grow to detest it.

Chance Encounters

Being single should never prevent anyone from enjoying and participating in events or activities of interest. In fact, going alone can be a terrific way to meet someone. These are venues such as art galleries and other places of interests, walks or bike rides in the park, and at the food market. Naturally, this makes good sense as it is a particularly good way to meet individuals with similar interests. Of course, we never want to go or participate in an activity under false pretenses as others we meet will rightly assume we are there because it is an activity that we enjoy and one in which we regularly engage. That wouldn't be truthful, and it is not a fair or wise choice.

As for the market, there are clues for compatibility right in our carts. Explore that. It is better than a blind date, and gives you some 'food for talk.' The other thing is that places like the supermarket offer fairly innocuous venues; be open to it.

Taking jobs that put you in touch with the Public

Everyone laughs about this as they see it as some sort of gold digging venture. It is not, although with something like bank tellering it does make it easy to get a handle on that kind of information on the prospect. There are many public positions, even as a volunteer, that allow us to meet individuals whom we are able to get to know on a fairly regular basis, become friends with first, and eventually begin to date. Our smile and body language should assist in communicating a message of interest.

Other opportunities include:

A Bar/Nightclub—As we know, this is a somewhat unpopular option, due to the superficiality component, but obviously can and has worked. If you are someone who can enjoy the conversation and dance offered at the bars, then go with that idea and no other expectation. If you find someone interesting, it won't be because that was your main objective of the evening.

At work, but could be risky and may be uncomfortable in the long run. Still, relationships are formed at work because we spend so much time there and it is a large factor in what we have in common. It offers an opportunity to get to know someone quite well before we establish anything further.

Taking classes in something you love…you're bound to find people with similar interests there.

We might even use **flirting** techniques when at a bookstore or library. If we are so inclined, this is a great way to connect with someone in a safe environment.

Remember, whatever choice we make, it will be important to smile in order to invite interest from others. And, since we never know who people know, at the very least we might find that someone knows someone we should meet.

We can be engaged in these kids of activities while remaining realistic about their limitations, and still pursue the more assertive means we discussed above. If we are serious about meeting people, just being out there exposes us potentially to others who are like us and share in our interests. Besides, we get to see them in action before they are on their best behavior during a first date!

Stage 4 The Interview...

The summary statement and resume only highlights what we have to offer, just like personals ads. This is what gets us in the door. Once we are inside, we need to "sell ourselves," first over the phone, and then during the face-to-face interview. And sales is a proper analogy. Just as employer and perspective employee are sizing up one another at that preliminary interview, there are similar evaluation dynamics that take place during our first date with someone. We will want to establish rapport, build trust, listen to their needs, and be able and willing to meet those needs, all while being mindful of our own. We are both trying to determine how suitable the match is so that we can go the next step. Otherwise, the only thing that 'closes' is the door.

Up until this point, we have been discussing what is understood to be the screening interview process. Talking to people over the phone during an initial contact and continuing on to the first date, is still only a screening exercise. The only difference in the first date is that we are face-to-face, and we have the benefit of a few things we didn't have over the phone. It probably won't be until the second date that we experience more in-depth interviewing activity that gets us deciding more serious issues. In the meanwhile, with voice personals dating at least, we can continue to have fun with screening all those prospects.

Preparing for the Interview

Someone recently told me that in training people how to interview for a job, she often poses this question to her participants: Wouldn't it have been great if we could have used these steps in getting to know our prospective spouse and determining whether there is a good fit?

If we have decided in the initial face-to-face that this person is someone to pursue, then we arrange a second date. It's usually a natural progression, but we should have some sort of a plan, particularly if we choose not to waste time.

One of the most important objectives is to get enough information about someone so that we can make a proper decision. If we do not have the time or occasion to accomplish that in the first interview, the second date is likely a good time. We do need to be prepared; what do we want to know, how can we ask questions that get us the information we need to gather together to make a proper assessment?

The more we need to know, the more we need to ask open-ended questions. These are questions that get our prospect to talk, to open up. "Tell me," "What do you think," and the whys and hows, all get someone responding in a fashion where we can gather additional information.

In a job interview scenario, we tell people that it is a two-way communication process where both parties engage to discover three things: Can this person do this job, How motivated are they to do what I need to have done, and Do they fit into the culture of this group or organization?

As we sit across from someone while on a date, each step of the conversation is being similarly evaluated by both persons. We are both asking ourselves:

- Who is this person?
- What do they want?
- How will they fit into my life?

The 'Who is this person' will answer identity questions like background, occupation, family, etc. We get a glimpse of what they do, what learning experiences they have acquired as they have lived their lives. The 'What do they want' question will get us information about their interests and motivations. What we know is that strong interests becomes psychological needs and must somehow be manifest in one's life. Knowing this may help us in deciding whether there is a match in what our date needs and what we need ourselves. It answers questions related to goals and values and offers hints about personality and temperament. If our values are congruent, the next thing we need to know is 'How' the individual fits in to our life just as they are. This is important because it is a culture issue that begs unconditional acceptance. The person we date, especially one with whom we intend to develop a relationship, needs to be at home with us as much as we need to be at home with them. Otherwise, this *lack of fit* will eventually surface as a problem, and one of us will opt out due to the discomfort we feel.

In the end, it looks like this:

If I can eventually love this person as they are—who they are, and I have some similar interests in the things they do, believe they are motivated to love and accept me, with common goals, values, and it makes sense to have us in each other's lives, then we have a promising relationship and possible future.

It is said that we never get a second chance to make a first impression and those initial impressions may be longer lasting than we care to acknowledge. That is why it is a good idea to consider putting our best foot forward, without being dishonest. There are certain things that we should be cognizant of during that initial face-to-face interview. First, consider that in our first meeting, there is our visual presentation, how we decide to dress and look for the occasion. Then, there is the verbal dialogue. We need to be concerned with how we come across during that first meeting, even as we want to portray as genuine a picture as possible. There's no need or pressure to lay all our cards out on the table, especially if we are still very much engaged in the exploration stage. Finally, there is the consideration of what we communicate about ourselves and about our feelings toward the one we are with, in non-verbal language.

Non-verbal Communication

The non-verbal "dialogue" is a particularly interesting dynamic in interpersonal relationships. Experts claim that as much as 55% of what gets communicated is accomplished non-verbally. That means that more important than what we say is all that other stuff, including eye contact, inflections, gestures, and smiles. It does sound like an awful lot, but don't worry, it all comes quite naturally. In fact, part of what we refer to as chemistry has to do with what is going on non-verbally between two people. We just need to understand that there are consequences to all those natural goings on; it is tied in to the 'flight or fight' adrenaline response. This is because messages received in this manner have power and can cause us to react either passively or aggressively.

We read one another non-verbally, whether or not we are conscious of it, and our body language gives us away if we are feeling negative for some reason. Scientists tell us that when we are feeling good with someone, pleasure chemicals are released within the body, which leave us with a natural high. We recognize this when we are first very attracted to someone, and we find we aren't hungry, going for long periods without eating or not requiring the sleep that we do normally.

Think of body language as our intuition. If someone is demonstrating negative body language toward us, it may be that they are struggling with an intuition that is begging for them to end the torture. And if we find ourselves exhibiting negative body language, know that somehow we feel it and the person we are with can sense it. It is a reliable source of feedback, even if we would rather not attend to what it is trying to tell us. But remember, non-verbal communication needs to be evaluated in gesture clusters, not in isolated segments. In other words, there needs to be congruency with multiple gestures before we interpret the intuitive message.

When it comes to dating and relationships, we are continually reading signals from each other. We aren't always consciously aware, nor are we always correct, but that's why we buy books like this. We want to raise our awareness and make us informed daters, rather than confused singles, fearful of getting back in the game. It's good to seek and get confirmation for what our gut already may have told us.

Stage 5 "The Close"

If we follow our sales analogy within the one of a job search, we understand that eventually we need to make a decision. This is true whether we are buying or selling. If we are selling, we want to know if someone is buying, and if we are the buyers, we want to have had all our questions answered before we decide. To some extent, it will depend upon our unique personalities, of course, but in general, we are buyers and sellers in the dating game.

Salespeople are taught that there are different types of closing techniques. For example, there is what is known as an assumptive close. This assumes you have the deal, and you'd just ask when or how the buyer would like to pursue it. Then there is the choice close, similar to the assumption in that you figure it's a done deal, all you now need to know is whether the buyer prefers choice a or b.

It's probably fair to say that if we are confident going in to a dating situation, we can assume that we have the interest of our date. And to some extent, we have closed the deal, if we indeed get to the first date after a "screening" telephone conversation. But, while this is the end of the cycle when we are selling widgets, it is only the beginning in what we call "relationship sales." In other words, the success of this preliminary close will set up the basis for the relationship, but by itself will neither sustain the relationship nor guarantee all future sales. We won't be able to relax; we will need to continue to cultivate the association with care and attention.

Here's something I once heard in reference to the closing a sale. It stayed with me, and I'm sure it'll make an impact on you: *If two people want to do business together, the details will never stop it from happening. If two people do not want to do business together, the details will never make it happen.* What that tells us is that in the end, people do business with people; they really want and maybe even need to like the person with whom they are doing business. In dating, we already know that's the case. People who want to date aren't going to let a few details get in the way of their being able to at least get together a few more times after the first date. If they do not want to date, if there isn't a mutual desire, the fact that someone's in an admired profession, makes a lot of money or is beautiful won't be enough to sustain the interest.

Getting to the close sometimes is a matter of accumulating a number of "yes" responses from the buyer. The idea is that if the seller does his job, he listened for what the buyer needs and verbalizes those needs back in the form of questions that are guaranteed to get an affirmative response. The buyer is placed in the natural position of agreement with the seller, and as long as the seller can deliver, a deal is consummated.

In dating and relationships, this technique is similar to mirroring. When we have done a good job of active listening, we have absorbed information in a way that makes the other person feel understood and not judged. Fundamentally, we are giving back what was said to us and asking for agreement. It causes the other person to feel safe with us and confident in the association. They trust us. When our feelings are this positive, and we literally cannot say no to what is being asked of us in confirmation of our own needs, how can we not "buy?"

On The Art of Flirting...

There are some of us who are great at this, and others of us who stink. If we are of the latter persuasion and wish to be of the former, it will need to be a conscious endeavor. For example, in speaking to a single woman,

I found that whenever she found a man attractive, she would automatically avoid eye contact, and never, ever, smile! She is aware that she is not good at flirting because she is terrified of it. Well, we hope for her sake, she wasn't expecting the object of her attraction to somehow *approach her*. Chances are that even if he *were* attracted to her, he wouldn't approach...not with the kind of body language she was transmitting!

For this woman, her act was conscious. It was the fear of rejection that precluded her from acting interested. God forbid she smiled at him and he walked away or ignored her! She believes in pain avoidance and has already convinced herself that the pain of potential rejection is far worse than the consequence of complete avoidance.

But, think about this for a minute. Wouldn't she have been better off attempting to show a bit of interest rather than to turn him away with such negative body language? Not only would she increase the chances of gaining a positive response-- having encouraged, rather than discouraged and possibly even disappointed him-- but she may have felt better about having taken action on something she wanted. Her way was almost a guarantee to send him running, where this way would have at least reassured him that he probably would not be rejected.

There is an art to flirting and it is nothing to be ashamed of or squeamish about. Here are six rules of flirting according to Dr. Judy Kuriansky who writes in *The Complete Idiot's Guide to Dating(1996):*

• Use flattery. Find something you like about the way a person looks or acts and compliment that. This isn't cajoling, she warns that it must be sincere.

• Become a good listener. Kuriansky calls undivided attention to the talker a "most powerful aphrodisiac," and I couldn't agree more.

• Discover which interests you have in common. It is a great way to start a conversation and always have something to talk about.

• Be responsible by taking care to be truthful and clear about your intentions. Try not to give anyone the wrong impression by what you do or say. Be sensitive to their feelings.

• Trust yourself enough to be able to flirt without negative consequences to your self-esteem. Don't consider it rejection if someone isn't interested, just move on to someone who invites your advances.

• Smile. Our smile is such an important part of letting someone know that we are interested and that they are being accepted.

Although I explained them in a slightly different context, the first letter of the underlined words spell out the word "flirts," to make it easier for us to remember. We need to also add complimentary body language gestures such as eye contact, facial expressions, postures, and even touching someone (in a non-sexual way, of course).

We really need to understand that flirting is not a bad thing. I spoke to numerous people who have assured me that they would welcome someone letting them know of an interest. They often feel they are involved in a constant guessing game. Remember, that if she's sitting there hoping he approaches her while he sits there considering if he should dare, nothing happens, and both people leave wondering.... Why let this happen?

♥ ♥ ♥

DateNotes

- ♥ Think of the search for a mate like going for that job that you know you would love, but do not do it without first understand ing how to set and achieve that goal.

- ♥ Be mindful of the "Be-Do-Have" theory of goal setting. First you have to be who you are in your head first, then you will naturally do the things that people like you do in order to have the things that you want in your life. You see, once you are the you in your head that you want and love to be, the "right" person, just like the "right" job somehow finds its way to you. But you have to believe it, and then *be it* before you can *have it.* It never works the other way around: we can never *have* (accumulating or otherwise) things that get us to *be* someone. Never. Think about it, and then you decide how you will personally work this in your own unique situation, as only you could make that determination.

- ♥ If it helps, use the principles of managing a solid job campaign to help you in meeting the person with whom you would like to spend time. After you acknowledge the stages of grieving, using your identified support network to help you, know that you are ready to move forward once you have gained acceptance and realize that all that happened was purposeful.

- ♥ You don't have the opportunity to select circumstances, but you can always choose your responses. Understand how powerful this is—you have the choice to either learn and grow or become a victim of circumstance and be destroyed. There's one old saying that helps many of us going through difficult times and that is, *if it doesn't kill you, it'll make you strong*. Choose wisely; choose strength.

- ♥ Objective self-assessment is an essential component for achieving happiness in what we do for a living as well as in who we date and eventually select for a life partner. But knowing who we are isn't only about who we are in our *heads*, the expectations someone else has of us, or even those expectations we have of ourselves because of the expectations someone (usually an important person in our lives) has for us. That counts, but only if when we count it we can release it when that happens to conflict with who we are in our *hearts*.

- ♥ Objective self-assessment says here's who I am (an identity), and here's who I *really* am (my deep psychological interests and needs) and here's the stuff that's in common. To the extent that what is in common is consistent with how that fits in with another person's life, with their values, goals, and philosophy, we may have a good match. To the extent that it fails to do that, we may be presented with challenges that will test the relationship.

If these are insurmountable challenges, the relationship may fail. And all this may have nothing at all to do with love, because remember, sometimes it won't be the love that goes, it'll be the relationship.

- Do not be afraid to try different ways to get yourself out there and meet other available people. When we are still in our twenties, it is somewhat easier to meet other singles on a regular basis, because our network during those years is most active with other singles. But once we get to an age where most of our friends are married, perhaps we work a job that keeps us very busy, and we meet few others. We are usually too tired to care once the weekend arrives, if we have not devised some kind of plan.

- We know that once we have actually been married and divorced, our network not only has shrunk due to having been out of the dating scene for some time, but we have developed to a different level. We may have children to consider, we may be substantial ly older, and/or our priorities may have shifted. What worked to meet people before doesn't quite work now. Besides, you may want to take advantage of options readily available today, but you hesitate due to lack of time, awareness, or confidence in relationships, in these new vehicles, or even in yourself. This last relationship could have shattered your self-confidence and the potential for rejection just does not sound appealing. Don't allow all these fears to rob you of the potential to re-connect and have fun.

- Instead of giving up on love and allow valuable time to pass while you are lonely, take the time you need to gain the acceptance we discussed in the grieving process, and then devise a plan. You will know when you are ready, and it will be so much better if you wait. Look in to the various vehicles to meet other singles and decide which one will work for you. Then, *just do it*!

- Sometimes it feels really good to just get out there again and talk to people who are interesting and interested in what you have to say and in who you are. It's definitely an ego boost, if nothing else. Take it slow, and don't expect a lot—that will put undue pressure on you and the other person. You don't want that. Go in to it with the idea that you will have fun, meet people, and possibly end up with a new friend or two. And then, see what happens. It could be the best thing you ever did. Be open to the possibilities!

- When you get to meet all those "new possibilities," remember that your initial dates (which aren't really dates, but interviews) are spent determining whether or not there is adequate interest in pursuing the association. If this sounds too technical or official or clinical for you, try to get over that because it does make practical sense.

- You are attempting to determine three things at the initial meet ing after your brief telephone conversation: Can we proceed, is this person who I like, where in life I like, etc., Is this person interested in similar things in terms of our views on important matters, values, goals, I don't know, raising children (shouldn't get that far on the first meeting, but who knows?), and finally, is this individual where I am culturally, do we "fit," is there enough common ground to suit one another. If you have green lights all the way, keep moving forward, but if not, nothing's lost at this point but an hour or two with another human being that you decided to meet and with whom you have shared a brief encounter. Just like the end of an initial job interview where one or both parties decide that it probably isn't going to work, you thank each other for the time, say good bye and wish one another well.

- Getting to the end of that first meeting with the big green light is indeed exciting and encouraging. You have successfully made a sale, bought time and a promise, closed the deal. The payoff is not financial, but it is emotional. There is hope, maybe only a friendship, but perhaps a chance at love. Although it is a "pre-liminary close," it is a promise of opportunity and you will take it. It feels good, even if it is somehow momentarily frightening. It means that you will see each other once again and take the potential to another level, if that is to be.

- Finally, do not be afraid to flirt. Flirting isn't at all synonymous with slutting (I know that's not a word, but it is a concept that I wish to convey). Whether you are a man or a woman, people rarely know that you are interested in them if you can not or refuse to at least give them some sign of your interest. Make it comfortable for you without betraying who you are. If you do nothing more than smile, that's okay. If a picture is worth a thousand words, then a smile is worth two thousand to you, particularly in the interest of conveying interest.

Three

ATTRACTION THEORIES

...Suddenly it isn't enough that their partners be affectionate, clever, attractive, and fun-loving. They now have to satisfy a whole hierarchy of expectations, some conscious, but most hidden from their awareness.
Harville Hendrix, Ph.D., *Getting the Love You Want*, p.54

On a surface level, attraction usually amounts to a physical one in the beginning. Two people look at each other and they decide whether they meet the surface criteria before they begin conversation. Personality is usually next in line, when we quickly assess whether or not the two of us have enough in common, whether we like their behavior, their discussion, the way they are with us. We ask ourselves questions like what is important to me, and does the other person feel similarly about that, and do they do the things that make me smile or cause me to scream. Usually, if we have the initial chemistry, we want to do it again. And each time we are with this person, we continue to learn about us as individuals and as a couple.

Fundamentally, each of us is attracted to people we like, people with whom we share some commonality, and to people who make us feel good about ourselves. If we happen to be emotionally healthy, these are usually the same people who are as emotionally healthy as we are.

Harville Hendrix who wrote, *Getting the Love You Want (1988)*, discusses three major theories of romantic attraction. From a basic biological perspective, men instinctively choose mates who will enhance the survival of the species. Theoretically, men would be concerned with childbearing capability in a woman and thus is drawn to those qualities that indicate robust health. This helps to explain man's attraction to youthful beauty, since there is some correlation between physical attributes and childbearing (pg. 5). Women, on the other hand, would tend to be more concerned with selecting someone who could provide, as the male dominance of primitive times ensured the survival of the family. And this is one of the explanations behind women's seeming attraction to men with money and power.

The social psychology theory is that we select our equals, based on physical, social, financial, and personality traits. This is a rationale that progresses from basic to a more holistic view of attraction. The "exchange theory" was supported by a study in 1986 in the New York Times reported by Daniel Goleman (author of *Emotional Intelligence*, 1995). The 537 dating men and women involved in the study were found to feel guilty and insecure when they viewed their partners as superior to them and angry when they viewed their partners as inferior. I guess that's why it is best to be with our *equals*.

Another idea suggests that we are attracted to individuals who most enhance our self-esteem. This is a theory that has us caring about what others think, as we need for our partner to be someone other people approve of, perhaps even envy. And Hendrix reminds us of the validity of this theory as each of us has felt pride or embarrassment at how our partners were perceived by others.

Still, these theories are inadequate as they fail to explain why and how each of us is attracted on a deeper level to only a few people in our lives. And why, ironically, those people all somehow tend to be similar. The explanation can only be found in our subconscious attractions. As Hendrix puts it: "It appears that each one of us is compulsively searching for a mate with a very particular set of positive and negative personality traits."

Renowned author and psychiatrist, M. Scott Peck, M.D., writes about relationships in his book, *A World Waiting To Be Born (1993).* He helps debunk the myth of the one perfect person theory, writing that there is no "someone special meant for us in our stars." But he says there is a force that causes us to attract. He admits this force to be an old reliable principle in psychiatry, that the best way to determine the severity of a patient's illness is by the company he or she keeps. He calls it a "profound tendency" for those similarly ill to hang out or associate with one another. Dr. Peck goes on to explain our attraction, or "choice":

The personalities of marital partners are often strikingly different, but their level of maturity is usually strikingly similar. ...Emotionally healthy ...tend to marry other healthy individuals, emotionally sick people to marry other sick people, and the in-between to marry in-betweens. This pattern of choice is as predictable as it is unconscious.

It is true that our subconscious plays a major role in our lives, dictating our attitudes and magnetic-like attractions. The reason this happens is because way back when we were so young that we could not know any better, we were developing our personalities and formulating our belief systems. Those belief systems were created by our thoughts and housed our self-concept, what we thought about ourselves, and our self-esteem, how we feel about ourselves. Once that was set, the resulting feelings dictated our attitudes, which manifested in our actions, the way we behave. So that our subconscious is at the root of who we become, what we need, and what we consequently attract.

There is some evidence questioning the "tabula rasa" (blank slate) notion, as we do enter life with some innate characteristics and essence. One of the best books to discuss this recently is *The Soul's Code*, by James Hillman (1996). We are, after all, live beings upon conception. Still, much of what has been discussed in terms of how we get to be who we are and what we attract comes from a fundamental learning experience. We know that we learn from impact and repetition, from observation and imitation. We have the strong influence of our caretakers and we understand how society does a fabulous job of teaching, even dictating value expectations and cultural norms. The transmission of this information is easily facilitated through regularly available media, sending us strong messages and serving to reinforce what we have already learned is acceptable and preferred. It is possible that these layers of learning have developed a life of their own and have obscured our original essence.

Our subconscious is a powerful driving force in our lives because it constitutes a major portion of our brain (thought to be as much as 88 percent). Besides that relatively unknown fact is the notion that our subconscious minds can not discern the difference between fact and fiction. This allows us to decide what we want our minds to believe and when we provide that information, it will simply obey those thoughts. It is an empowering notion of which few of us take full advantage.

Why do we continue to meet women/men "just like" dear mom or dad?

The unconscious selection process has brought together two people who can either hurt each other or heal each other, depending upon their willingness to grow and change. (p131)

Harville Hendrix, Ph.D.
Getting The Love You Want, 1988

Once we know how we *naturally* draw people into our lives who most closely resemble our past, what is familiar, we are not so surprised to find ourselves repeating patterns of attraction. Not only does our first love seem strangely like our father with whom we had issues, but after that romance ended, our second relationship involves the 'same' man with a different name and shoe size.

Parents influence us by their example. They teach us how to live and love by what we see them do. We go on to select a mate based on that model, whether or not we consciously accept it, and it often becomes a concealed source of tension in our relationships. The problem is that we end up being more influenced by our caretakers' negative traits.

Whenever there are unresolved childhood issues, we continue to create the circumstances that will allow us another opportunity to replay that scene. *This time* we know we'll get it right. *This* time, we *will* resolve it. In an effort to control things this time, things which we once felt were out of our control, we draw in those people that will help us accomplish the re-creation. Who better to help us with it than people *just like* our family, just like those with whom we have unfinished business? On a less-than-conscious level, it is our chance to fix it.

While it is probably not so bad if we continue to meet, date, fight, and break up with these attractions, it is a very bad idea to enter into a marital arrangement with these props. If dating and experimenting is the dress rehearsal, marriage is the real deal. It's too tough to exit once we have made that sort of a legally binding decision.

We think and we question...

Why do I get to meet all the JERKS? Am I wearing a sign that says "All Jerks Welcomed?"

Well, truth is, we may not exactly be wearing a sign in *print*, but we're probably wearing it all over our face, in a manner of speaking. We send out signals, emit vibes to others all the time -- through what we wear, where we go, what we do, the things we say, even the line of work we have chosen. It's like the Ralph Waldo Emerson quote that says: "*What you are speaks so loudly that I cannot hear what you say*." Again, what we do so well, is that *our* subconscious attracts the subconscious of another person who presents the greatest opportunity for us to reconnect with our past. We are *familiar* with this; it is our comfort zone.

The obvious problem with such a dynamic is that it is not always positive. We may be challenging ourselves to once again resolve the unresolvable. Our recreation is motivated by the subconscious desire to "play it out," like in a theater. If we place everything back to the way "it" happened, props and all, perhaps this time the outcome will be different. You see, this time, I know *better*. It's as if we really believe that we can change what we didn't like--make it all better, happy--the way it "should" have been.

We can attract all the people in the world that would supply us with the proper scenario. If they are "Jerks," it is because we are sending out those kinds of attraction signals. (It is our interpretation, anyway; the designation of jerk is one that we assign. It's a judgment, and it may be projection.) Resolution will not be ours, however, until we see and accept our past as it was and acknowledge its place in our history. Just as we cannot bring back the dead, we cannot resurrect our past to change it. It was what it was. It is what it was. The interesting thing that happens when we finally figure this out is that we no longer need to attract the past once we accept it. We are free to go on, attracting what we *desire* in our lives, not what we need to fix or correct.

Remember that definition of insanity that is often used in getting people to cease engaging in unhealthy choices: *doing the same thing over and over and expecting different results.* If we continue this cycle of re-creation, the only thing we can hope for is the same disappointing results. And that leaves us feeling powerless, victims again, of the same unfortunate (past) situation. Because while the names and faces may change, the drama we recreate continues to lead us to the same, sometimes tragic conclusion.

This should not leave us feeling hopeless and helpless. On the contrary, it is an empowering piece of information. We no longer have to feel as if there *is* anything to overcome. What was simply is; there is nothing to change, nothing to do about it. In fact, it was a perfect experience for us to become who we are and all that we were meant to be. Lessons learned are the gifts we pass on to our future and that is hopeful.

Acceptance of what is and was enables us to move freely forward. The coast is clear. We won't need to keep attracting "past potentials" any longer. We are now open to attracting those who meet with our *latest* and *revised* dominant thoughts: The ones that say we're worth it, we count, we're pretty darned wonderful.

And that's not conceit; it is not obnoxious or repugnant. It is pure unadulterated self-love. Something that without, we are free to love no one.

Continuing to repeat the issues of the past, even with only a subconscious attempt at resolution, ensures that we relive the pain. And these occasions will persist in arising until we learn precisely what they are here to teach us. "Opportunities" will continue to tap us on the shoulder, as if to say, *'hey, you don't get the message yet, so here's another chance.'* This is because although the form may change, the content (our lesson) will always be the same. The temporary disguise may fool us, but we eventually see it for what it is--our same old problem. We know we finally 'got it' when our issue stops presenting itself and that pain is no longer there.

It is easy to see how and why we are often in relationships that are not so healthy. We are with someone far too long or with far too much intensity. Some of us go all the way into destructive attraction patterns.

It's no wonder why so many of us are frustrated with the whole idea of dating or finding a life partner. We're ready to give up and live alone. But it doesn't have to be that way.

Understanding how we are attracted to someone helps us avoid bad situations and attract good ones. But it will take time to change the way we think. It will take whatever time necessary to have a consciousness about it, so that we are able enough and strong enough to let it go. The force can be intense because we have an innate desire to redo our past and make it be what we think it should have been. Our "automatic pilot" is often comprised of non-productive behavior patterns that we have learned. We are reacting, so it takes conscious effort and the strength of desire to want to respond more productively and change these patterns. It gets back to our subconscious honing in on someone else's subconscious and they get to agree on what the relationship is going to look like. One thing is sure: until we have independently pursued the work on ourselves, we cannot hope to be healthy inside a relationship, nor are we likely to even attract the appropriate person. John Gray, Ph.D., author of the popular, *Men are From Mars, Women are From Venus*, wrote:

> *...the best way to find your soul mate is to give up searching for your soul mate, and instead focus on preparing yourself so that you can recognize your soul mate when he or she appears. When you are ready, your soul mate will appear.*

Opposites Attract Theory

There is some reason to believe that attractions may have some link to DNA. We may have greater attractions to people who are most unlike us in their genetic makeup. This is said to be due to our drive and search for a good combination of genes in procreation.

A similar opposites attract theory is at work in terms of character traits. Most of us are attracted to someone who possesses qualities different from us. For example, if we tend to do things spontaneously, we might be more attracted to a more cautious individual, one who needs to think through before he or she acts. If we enjoy going out to big social gatherings, we might have a mate who would rather spend a quiet evening at home. If we like to spend money, we may be with someone who is frugal. If we are one of those self-sacrificing people, we probably have someone who is more self-involved. If we are logical and precise, we may be with someone who uses emotion and intuition. Type A people who may exhibit signs of anxiety could likely be attracted to a more relaxed individual. And so on. The point is, as we will discuss in the next chapter on assessing compatibility, we all need to appreciate our mates for who they are and what they offer us in terms of temperamental balance. This is another example of how we have many opportunities to learn from one another.

The only "F" word that scares us Loveless

There is routine agreement among psychologists and holistic thinkers that *fear* is the only negative emotion there is. In relationships, it's no different. Fear is what causes us to put up walls and distance ourselves from our partner; fear is the reason behind our inability to calmly discuss our issues, concerns, and reveal the innermost parts of ourselves. And fear is what motivates some of us to marry, cheat, divorce, and isolate ourselves. We are afraid of intimacy, afraid of losing, of hurting, and of loving. Most psychologists will agree that negative emotion, whether it is jealousy, anger, resentment, or guilt, originates from *fear*.

This fear is an imagined barrier that comes to us disguised as these other feelings, but is here to alert us to something we need address in ourselves. In other words, once again, it is not about the other person; it is only about us. It is present to tell us about ourselves. And if we listen, it will reveal what is under our surface emotion and teach us a good deal. But if we fail to attend, if we deny or ignore or take cover with drinking, or drugging, eating, or working too much, then we will sabotage this great self-revelation being presented to teach us. It will motivate us to act from it, without having served its useful (positive) instructional purpose.

The real problem, of course, is that there is no resolution in succumbing to fear's hold on us. Its tactics will block access to love in our life. It cuts us off from feeling, and ultimately from our intuition, our inner guidance.

Do not let this happen. We have a choice. We can not allow fear, this "false evidence appearing real," scare us loveless. When we are experiencing a negative emotion, we must go inside and ask: *What am I afraid of?* And then be willing to listen for the answer. It takes time, patience, and a belief in oneself.

Take it one step further. We have the fear of rejection, the fear of commitment, the fear of failure. We sometimes hear of the fear of abandonment, the fear of losing control, and the fear of loss period. But think about it. Behind each of these fears is the unknown, isn't it? These fears should all be re-worded to be called ignorance. We're not afraid of rejection, we fear that our feelings will not be reciprocated and we just don't know that that's okay, that we will not only live through it, but also be better off because we deserve *mutual* love. Here we are encased in self-sabotage, when all we need is to reassure ourselves that we won't die if something bad happens. And when we refocus on what we want to have happen, we won't be predisposed to wallow in our sorrow.

♥ ♥ ♥

DateNotes

- We are indeed attracted to others based on some very superficial criteria, as they are attracted to us. We say that he or she is "my type," as we acknowledge our tendency to be captivated by a particular look. Still, we tend to be attracted to these "types" within the context of our psychological needs, as well. The people we end up with are usually the people with whom we need to learn or heal. While this isn't necessarily a bad thing, it can be very frustrating if we fail to recognize the lessons.

- If we can accept that it is our responsibility and no one else's to make us happy, we won't be so inclined to blame others. We will feel empowered because of our understanding that we can do something about our unhappiness.

- Happiness is not dependent upon circumstance or any other person in our lives; it is a choice we make. Remember that. It will help you feel in control of your life.

- Know that what we feel about ourselves on the inside will always manifest itself on the outside. If you are attracting the "wrong" person, you are doing and feeling something "wrong" and can correct it.

- Try not to resort to name-calling; referring to someone as a "jerk" hurts you as well as them. We aren't bad people, we are people who sometimes do bad things. Learn to separate the behavior from the person, and know that if someone is acting "jerky," they are hurt and looking to heal. Perhaps they are calling out for you to help them. We are intermittently teacher and student in all of life.

- ♥ Opposites often do attract. It creates nice balance in personality aspects. An individual who tends to be light and perhaps flighty likes and may even need someone who is well grounded. Someone who is a spendthrift usually finds it is convenient when his or her mate is frugal. Most of us find we are attracted to people who possess traits that we ourselves lack.

- ♥ You always have a choice on perspective. You can either choose to be motivated by fear or by desire. Coming from a negative point of view, we do things out of fear, while turning that around to be positive allows us to be motivated by what we want in our lives.

- ♥ If you question something you are doing, stop and ask yourself why, what thought or feeling motivated the action. If it is fear, turn it around to view it from the opposite perspective of desire. That has the effect of changing the thought you have about it and causing a more permanent change in the way you think.

Four

ASSESSING COMPATIBILITY

In the early 1900's, the famous Swiss Psychoanalyst, Carl Jung, identified four functions of consciousness and postulated that our behavior can be measured in generally one of several basic patterns. We have what he referred to as a preferred or dominant style, dictating our basic personality, describing how we go about getting our individual needs met. When our needs are not met, we experience what is called stress. It is the way we react when we feel we are losing control. Essentially, we would describe our behavior as productive when our needs are met by our environment, while we quickly adopt a non-productive behavior pattern when our needs cease being met by our environment.

Jung named the functions of consciousness Intuition, Thinking, Feeling, and Sensation. For the purposes of the exercise here, Intuition is the Creator, Thinking is the Evaluator, Feeling is the Persuader, and Sensation is the Doer.

Unlike in the area of values, we have already mentioned that it is possible to be somewhat different than our lifetime partners where temperament is concerned. While *too* much difference can present many challenges to a relationship, some difference may allow for some balance.

Let's have a little fun taking a look at our communication preferences or styles and how that might interact with a prospective mate.

Answer these several questions as honestly as you possibly can by placing a check mark after each description that most applies to you. This will determine your location on the scale identifying your dominant style. Please remember that there are no right or wrong answers; I have done my best not to use language that could be construed as judgmental. None of the instruments designed to describe personality is ever intended to be a measure of better or worse, simply different.

This particular questionnaire has not been scientifically validated. Nevertheless, it is my personal version of all of the various assessment instruments I have administered and used over the course of at least ten years. Remember, the results are not prescriptive, rather they are descriptive of our styles and patterns.

Enjoy it. Give enough thought to consider which description most applies to you, but don't belabor it with *too* much thought. You should be able to relate to one or the other relatively quickly. Trust your gut responses to the questions.

QUESTIONNAIRE 1A

Place a check on the line that best describes you; Col A represents the part of the question and Col B represents the second part of the ques

	Col A	Col B
1. Would you say your movements are (A) fast and instinctive OR (B) more slow and deliberate?	______	_____
2. Are you more of a (A) doer OR more of a (B) thinker	______	_____
3. Do you prefer (A) many casual acquaintances OR (B) the company of a few close friends	_____	_____
4. When making most decisions, do you (A) respond rather quickly OR do you (B) believe that you need time and information?	______	_____
5. Is your eye contact (A) intense and more constant OR is it (B) less intense and less consistent?	______	_____
6. Do you tend to (A) make your presence known OR are you (B) more comfortable 'behind the scenes'?	______	_____

6. Do you believe you are (A) more of a risk taker OR are you (B) more cautious in your approach to risks? ______ _____

7. Are you mostly (A) "bottom line" driven OR do you consider yourself (B) more interested in the process? ______ _____

9. Are you more likely to (A) confront/ take charge of a situation OR prefer the (B) step-back-and-wait approach? ______ _____

10. Under stress, might you become more (A) impulsive OR (B) less decisive? ______ _____

11. Are you more likely to (A) be motivated by a desire to affect people's lives OR (B) not so likely to be motivated? ______ _____

12. Would you describe yourself as a (A) keen observer OR (B) not terribly observant? ______ _____

13. Do you believe you are (A) considered to be more friendly OR (B) slightly more reserved? ______ _____

14. If you were a bird, which bird would you be? (A) an eagle OR (B) a dove? ______ _____

Sub Totals Col A (MA) ____ Col B (LA) ____

QUESTIONNAIRE 2A

In each pair, select the one meaning that most appeals to you:

	Col A		Col B
1. Persuasive	____	Introspective	____
2. Take-Charge	____	Reticent	____
3. Talk	____	Listen	____
4. Action	____	Contemplative	____
5. Spontaneous	____	Deliberate	____
6. Decisive	____	Inclusive	____
7. Energetic	____	Reserved	____
8. Direct	____	Plan	____

Totals Col A (MA)____ Col B (LA) ____

Questionnaire 1R

Now, answer these questions in terms of what is MOST like you:

	Col A	Col B
1. When you speak, do you (A) find that you do are NOT very animated OR that you (B) gesture frequently?	______	_____
2. Would you describe your movements as (A) fairly rigid OR (B) more free and less rigid?	______	_____
3. Do you have (A) little facial expression OR (B) more facial expressiveness?	______	_____
4. Do you appear (A) more serious OR (B) more willing to play?	______	_____
5. Is your dress more (A) formal OR (B) casual, less formal?	______	_____
6. Would you describe yourself as (A) practical and rational OR more (B) unstructured and introspective?	______	_____
6. Do you tend to (A) control your feelings OR are you (B) less guarded and likely to say whatever you feel?	______	_____

7. Are you more (A) detail-oriented OR do you (B) tend to rely on the 'big picture'? ______ _____

8. Do you feel you generally (A) tend to focus on tasks OR are you (B) definitely more people-oriented? ______ _____

10. How do you make decisions...(A) using facts OR (B) relying more on your feelings and gut instincts? ______ _____

11. Would you describe yourself as (A) more structured with time OR (B) less so? ______ _____

12. Is your "supervisory" style generally (A) disciplined and objective OR (B) more personal in nature? ______ _____

13. Would you rather (A) have a plan for what you are doing for the day OR do you (B) prefer spontaneity? ______ _____

14. If you were a bird, which bird would you be? (A) An owl OR a (B) peacock? ______ _____

Sub Totals Col A (LR) ____ Col B (MR) ____

Questionnaire 2R

In each pair, select the one meaning that most appeals to you.

	Col A		Col B
1. Serious	____	Playful	____
2. Facts	____	Feelings	____
3. Concrete	____	Global	____
4. Scheduled	____	Unplanned	____
5. Reasonable	____	Captivating	____
6. Conservative	____	Casual	____
7. Equity	____	Mercy	____
8. Factual	____	Theoretical	____

Totals Col A (LR) ____ Col B (MR) ____

Now go ahead and total your two scores on each set of the two questionnaires. The first set, questionnaires 1A and 2A, reveals your *assertiveness* component. If your total score is highest on the left, that means that you prefer to communicate in a *more assertive* manner. If your score is higher on the right side, it means that you tend to prefer a *less assertive* style. This also corresponds with what we know to be extroversion and introversion. The more assertive types would likely be those persons who get their energy from an externally dynamic environment (extroverted). Those whose preferences are less assertive or introverted, are energized more by their internal system.

The second survey, 1R and 2R, describes your *responsiveness* preference. If you scored highest on the left, it means that a *less responsive* description is most accurate for you. If your score is higher on the right side, it means that you tend to be *more responsive* in your style. This component also has a corresponding reference, with less responsive persons tending toward greater objectivity and task-orientation, and more responsive individuals preferring a personalized approach, greater emphasis on people.

Here are the definitions in the context of this non-validated assessment instrument:

ASSERTIVENESS describes our readiness to exert power or control over other people.

RESPONSIVENESS describes how disposed we are to express our own feelings and emotions.

A More Assertive/ More Responsive (upper right quadrant) individual we will call a PERSUADER. These people enjoy talking and are people-oriented as well as results-oriented. They make good salespeople, teachers, managers, and retailers. They may work in public relations or human resources. They enjoy pleasing others, so they will generally tend to conform to the dress within their environment, with some flair to show off their friendly personality and individuality.

A Persuader would be easy to meet and to talk to. Although they can be take-charge types, they have a tendency to be sensitive to the needs of others. If you meet a Persuader, it's likely that you'll find them accessible and somewhat charismatic. If you are a Persuader, remember to listen as much as you possibly can; you'll learn more (about others) sooner that way. If you'd like to meet a Persuader, smile and become a good listener.

Since we want to address these styles from the aspect of needs, we want to recognize the Persuader as interested in harmony and balance. Since they are likely to be concerned with what other people think, we mustn't view that as a character flaw, rather a requirement of their nature.

A More Assertive/Less Responsive (upper left quadrant) style is predominately a DOER. This is an individual who has a sense of urgency in getting things done. They are task and fact-oriented and decisive. They make good 'bottom line' managers and can be self-employed. They will dress more conventionally, but are not be terribly concerned with sartorial perfection. A DOER moves quickly, so minute details are often not high priority.

A no-nonsense Doer type may be more difficult to meet than the more engaging Persuaders. Still, since they are loyal, committed, and reliable, they make good lifetime partners. If you happen to be a Doer, you may want to be mindful of appearing distant or even abrupt to a prospective partner. If you‘d like to meet a Doer, you should probably take the direct approach; he or she would appreciate that.

The take-charge nature of the Doer may mean that if they get the proper signal, they will not waste any time asking someone out or pursuing the relationship straight on. They are not likely to lead someone on if they have no interest. It simply wastes precious time and resources. They require little to no small talk, unlike the Persuader, who may enjoy that. When stress becomes a factor, however, it is possible that they can come across gruff and impersonal. Don't be overly sensitive; remember that they are meeting their own needs for expediency.

A Less Responsive/Less Assertive (lower left quadrant) individual is an EVALUATOR. This is a person who thinks through the detail, is organized and methodical. Often they are accountants, attorneys and engineers. They can be computer experts or scientists. EVALUATORS like plentiful information, preferring to rely on data to make difficult decisions. They are generally orderly and will tend to dress most conventionally of all the types.

Since Evaluators are often quiet and reserved, they may not be so easy to meet. They also may tend to go slower as their mode of operation is to think long and hard about making big decisions. But once they are in a relationship, they too can make enduring, faithful partners.

Because of their analytical nature, Evaluators can appear critical, inflexible, or indecisive, even as they are only going about getting their needs met. If you are an Evaluator, it might behoove you to relax and smile a bit more, to be cognizant of messages you may unwittingly convey to others that would put them off, particularly when you are attempting to draw them near. If you want an Evaluator to notice you, be somewhat businesslike and give them lots of information.

The Less Assertive/More Responsive (lower right) combination reveals a CREATOR type. These folks commonly engage in imaginative and original activities. Comfortable in the world of the abstract and conceptual, they are typically artists, inventors, even strategic planners, or marketers. They tend to prefer an unstructured environment where ideas can be generated. Dress for CREATORS can be rather original as they tend not to be conventional types.

Creators both fascinate and frustrate those of us who can not identify with them. They can attract many people, although that may not be an objective. The tendency to be internally driven almost precludes their concern with the opinion of others. Not meaning to discount the value of others, they simply tend to have a fair amount of curiosity and come across unrealistic or impractical.

A Creator could prove to be the most challenging of all types in terms of romantic involvement, as they have their own definitions for what is regularly accepted in conventional wisdom. Because the CREATOR lives in a world of possibilities, they may be very accepting of differences, in fact, intrigued by them. Constantly questioning and theorizing, they are not so willing to fall in line. If you think you are in love with a

Creator, you should probably be prepared to have long tangential, intellectual discussions. And you must be absolutely willing to be open-minded and as comfortable with them as they are with themselves. If you are a creator, try to remember that everyone who fails to share in your sense of wonder is not shallow or stupid, simply more concrete and involved in the world of reality. Consider how the two of you could effectively learn from one another and develop the perfect solution to a problem.

COMMUNICATION STYLES

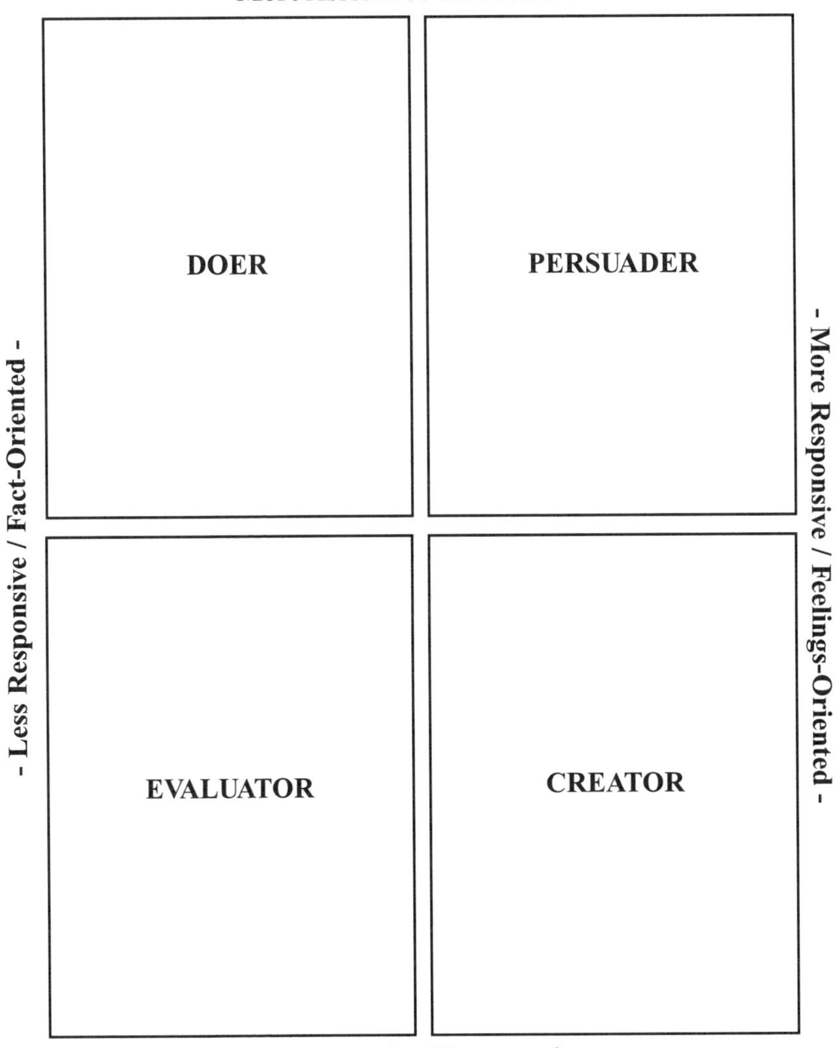

It's time to talk about compatibility. The fact is that all of us possess and use various aspects of each of these four basic styles. There are actually sixteen variations of these communication preferences, depending upon where you specifically fall within the quadrants. We merely conducted a cursory, unscientific query. You may want to pursue one of the validated instruments if you are after greater specificity. The two with which I am most familiar are the Myers Briggs Type Inventory (MBTI) and the Birkman Method.

All preferences are available to us and generally used by us at one time or another. We simply have predominance, or preference, for one or another. You may be interested and wondering where we get such tendencies. The source for how we develop these style preferences is most likely, like so much else, shared by nature and nurture. It is my personal belief that the more we examine our sources, the more we understand the role that nature plays in this. But for now, we will rest with the notion that we are born with a certain set of characteristics, and those characteristics are either encouraged or discouraged by our environment, which either maximize or minimize the propensity for those characteristics to express themselves in our lives.

Each of us possesses unique needs and each of us goes about getting those needs met in a different way. We respond to stress in unique ways, too. And there is no judgment about these varying needs, no good or bad needs, they simply are. That is why it is helpful to us to acknowledge our own and to whatever extent possible, be sensitive to the needs of the people in our lives.

Some of us are more adaptable in style differences than others of us. If your scores were, for example, far apart, say of the possible 22 points on Assertiveness, you were 20 Less Assertive; 2 More Assertive, it is more certain that you prefer to operate in a reserved, less dominating style. On the other hand, if your scores were closer, say, 10 for Less Assertive and 12 for More Assertive, you may use both styles almost equally in responding to your environment and getting your needs met.

When your scores indicate a negligible difference in your preference for one style or another, the good news is that this can indicate a greater tendency toward adaptability. So that you might exhibit some assertiveness, and at other times act in ways that are more characteristic of a less assertive style. The bad news is that because of this obvious flexibility, it may appear that you lack an identifiable focus, particularly if the Responsiveness component scores in a similar way (small difference between scores in less responsive/more responsive). Closeness in scores may also mean that you have more difficulty in making certain kinds of decisions also, perhaps such as with a career selection, or even in selecting a mate. The world of choice opens up to you, making it more difficult to choose or to feel very strongly one way or another. While those more definitive profiles with high score differences can be perceived as more rigid, one can easily see how they may also appear focused and decisive.

So how is this information helpful to those of us engaged in a mate search, or simply dating? To be sure, it is helpful to know who we are first, before inviting another to share in our lives. It is a tool used to raise our consciousness about our fundamental needs and behavior styles, providing clear, tangible information so that we are not fooling ourselves or anyone else about what we are made of. Perhaps the only reason that we would portray a less than accurate picture of ourselves is because we lack this kind of self-awareness, or because we believe that the real us is somehow flawed and unacceptable.

But the truth is that we are all flawed and all acceptable. We are flawed people loving other flawed people, and chances are that our behavior flaws are not the same ones. It works well in balancing that way, remember? The goal isn't to change the flaw but to gain acceptance, of ourselves and of others, just as they are.

If there is a specific behavior issue that gets in the way of our peaceful relationship with another, we will indeed be able to address that, but only if we personally want to change. "Correction" takes place when we make the decision based on the sincere desire along with a commitment to accommodate that loving relationship. But this is behavioral change, and not a change of our essence. In the end, we always need to accept another, even if we choose not to be with them.

The other benefit to this kind of awareness is that in acknowledging our differences, we are better able to depersonalize what someone says or does to us. For example, when our mate acts in ways that cause us to hurt, we might consider that there was no deliberate thought or malice intended, but rather that he or she had been attempting to meet a need. When we change the way we look at it and respond, rather than react, we establish a relationship where mutual love and support can thrive. We won't be constantly challenged by what are often insurmountable obstacles and challenges.

People least like us would appear in the style diagonally across from ours. Particularly if we score a strong type, that is, with the larger differences between the two numbers on either scale, these are people who think most unlike us. We share the least commonality, as they have neither scale in common with us. This does not mean that we cannot hope to get along with these people, nor should it mean that we mustn't date them, it simply says that we will likely not come from a very similar perspective on things. While some may see this as something to avoid, it may prove to be a great strength between two people. We need to decide for ourselves, but the key is to be aware, sensitive to another's needs. And we must not have unrealistic expectations, particularly when it comes to wanting to change someone over to our way of thinking.

How Style Differences Attract

As we mentioned earlier, the "opposite's attract" theory that contains an element of truth is with temperament. It is good to have some balance in personality for the couple's purposes as well as when they are joined by their children. Too much of one type can provide too much of one disposition and not enough of another.

We already discussed the importance of being similar in values and close in goals when it comes to a life partner. When it comes to personality, differences help maintain a balance in the complex of mental and emotional qualities that distinguish an individual.

As we have also noted, the quadrant diagonals may be the ones presented with the most challenging liaison. This is primarily because they share no real preference in common. In other words, they are entirely disparate in both characteristic components, assertiveness and responsiveness. The adjacent styles have a greater likelihood of compatibility. Still, this is all dependent upon how close or different the numbers are between the two opposing measures. So that someone who scores dramatically different between say, more assertive and less assertive, is more one or the other. Whereas an individual who scores close, perhaps within a 4-point difference, is less dramatic and therefore, less likely to be one way or the other, and more a combination of both.

Thus when we examine their positions, it is clear to see how the Persuader would have least similarity with the Evaluator, and the Doer the least similarity with the Creator. This again, is not to say that these relationships are impossible. You may know of some people who fit these types and live just fine together. It only means that there is a likeliness that the one style would have difficulty understanding the other, posing some communication challenges that would not be there were they more similar.

That being said, those styles that share one side of the quadrant, that is those adjacent to one another, would have a greater likelihood of sharing personality characteristics. For that reason, it may be that there is enough of a difference and still less of a challenge in simply getting along and understanding one another.

These are generalities, as we have already mentioned. Completing a questionnaire of this sort is both fun and interesting. It can provide you with greater insight to yourself and others for use as another tool in looking at compatibility.

Nevertheless, one would not want to give such a questionnaire to a prospective mate too early on in the relationship or in an effort to make a finite decision on compatibility. Actual experience will better assist us in determining the answers to such serious questions. Just as it would be unrealistic (and illegal, anyway) to use a personality assessment as the sole criterion for hiring in a work situation, it is likewise not advisable to use it exclusively in choosing a lifetime partner.

Behavior Under Stress

Whatever our predominant behavior style, we act in what we call a productive way when our needs are being met by our environment. But that doesn't always happen. Sometimes our needs are not being met and this causes us to react. We know that reactions are not productive behavior; they are rather stress behaviors, or non-productive.

Below is a list of positive characteristics and listed across from them are the negative version of those characteristics indicating what may happen when we are stressed.

CHARACTERISTICS ASSOCIATED WITH THE FOUR COMMUNICATION STYLES

EFFECTIVE	NON-PRODUCTIVE
INTUITOR	
original	unrealistic
imaginative	"far out"
creative	fantasy-bound
broad-scaled	scattered
charismatic	devious
idealistic	out-of-touch
intellectually tenacious	dogmatic
ideological	impractical
THINKER	
effective communicator	verbose
deliberative	indecisive
prudent	over-cautious
weighs alternatives	over-analyzes
stabilizing	unemotional
objective	non-dynamic
rational	controlled and controlling
analytical	over-serious, rigid

FEELER

spontaneous	impulsive
persuasive	manipulative
empathetic	over-personalizes
grasps traditional values	sentimental
probing	postponing
introspective	guilt-ridden
draws out feelings of others	stirs up conflict
loyal	subjective

SENSER

pragmatic	doesn't see long-range
assertive, directional	status seeking, self-involved
results-oriented	acts first, then thinks
technically skillful	lacks trust in others
objective-bases opinions	perfection-seeking
on what he actually sees	

Do People Change?

Personality has been defined as a consistent pattern of integration (or system) of psychic elements. ...The personality inherently resists change. People who come to psychotherapy do saying that they want to change, and then from the moment therapy starts they usually begin acting as if the last thing on God's earth they want to do is change.

M. Scott Peck, M.D.
A World Waiting To Be Born(1993)

Our personalities are so firmly rooted in our fundamental belief systems, that it is indeed difficult for us to change. We have an automatic pilot driven by our subconscious that begs consistency. The only change that becomes possible emanates from a sincere desire to change by the individual. This necessitates a change in the belief system, not merely a cosmetic change. In other words, there must be a compelling drive to change, the individual must accept first that their thinking needs to change. This sets off the feelings that created the attitude that led to the behavior. Any permanent change in our behavior will always be preceded by a corresponding change in our self-image and self-esteem.

♥ ♥ ♥

DateNotes

If your personality style happens to be a **DOER:**

- ♥ Remember that you need to make an effort to listen to others; this is particularly important on a first date.
- ♥ Because you tend to be fast-paced and results-oriented, you may cause stress in others, who are not quite that way. Exercise patience and enjoy the balance that someone different can provide.
- ♥ It will definitely increase your date's comfort level if you try to understand what he or she wants; acknowledge their suggestions and ideas.

If you are more of a **PERSUADER:**

- ♥ You will probably need to demonstrate some restraint of your impulses in order not to cause concern in others who have interest in you.
- ♥ Since you tend to act and decide quickly, remember that some people will need to be able to think more and take more time. Remain sensitive to these differences and allow them the consideration they need.

- Your risk-orientation and fact-orientation can put people off who are less risk and fact-oriented than you may be. Just acknowledge that and be mindful of the difference. It's actually a good balance.

- It is possible that your high energy, verbal fluency, and louder voice could intimidate others, even though it may be the reason that someone is attracted to you. Just try to be aware of this and do what you can to ease their fears.

- Remember to check your facts before you make decisions.

- Try not to speak until others have completed what they want to say and make a conscious attempt to become a good listener. The ability to listen is a very appealing characteristic in a partner.

- With many people, it will be fine for you to take center stage (as it takes the heat off them), but it would be nice to have you consider sharing the limelight on occasion.

To **CREATORS:**

- Since you have a tendency to be more passive in the dating arena, you may need to stretch yourself in demonstrating self-determination to get what you really want.

- Make an effort to set and achieve goals you want to achieve in a relationship.

- Don't dodge issues, rather try to let others know where you stand—avoid keeping them hanging.

If you are more of an **EVALUATOR:**

- Because of your need for lots of information, you appear indecisive to some others. Try to make quicker decisions and take action, especially in dating someone.

- Try not to be suspicious of someone who is different and needs you to make a decision, perhaps even pushes you to do so. Understand that this may be a need for them.

- Remember that someone who is not as organized and precise as you are is not necessarily scatterbrain and unintelligent. Everyone's unique worth just comes packaged differently and although the content is good, the form may look odd, especially to someone who is very systematic and methodical.

Five

THE GENDER DIFFERENCE

Resolution (of misconstrued communication between men and women), requires first becoming aware of how men and women differ biologically and psychologically, and then seeing how these differences are culturally magnified and distorted.

Harville Hendrix, *Keeping The Love You Find*, (1992) p.176

Communication preference assessments have built within their construct an allowance for what is referred to as a "gender bias." In other words, because of the tendency for males to respond in a particular way and for females to respond in another particular way, the questionnaires are put together to ensure a level field where scores are most accurately reflective of the individual.

A man is said to have a greater propensity to be "left-brained" because of his intrinsic need for power and control. Men tend to be task and object-oriented, interested in news and sports. Their competitive spirit allows them to enjoy the opportunity to prove something. They need approval and acceptance. A women is said to more likely possess "right brain" tendencies, highlighting needs that are more about harmony and communication. She needs to express and is likely to be feelings and people-oriented. She nurtures, and enjoys working to make something better.

We have regularly been made aware of communication problems between the sexes. Men do this, women think that. We usually manage, but sometimes we get into real trouble. When someone offends us, we might retaliate by attacking or withdrawing. Neither of those reactions gets us satisfaction because there is no communication. And we still have the problem, only next time, it'll be bigger, because we carry the residual anger over from the first time. Men and women have been engaged in this dance for some time, many with little hope of changing the way they communicate.

That's why books and materials that explain things like the different languages between the sexes and cultural differences between men and women are met with almost immediate popularity. We want to know, we need to figure this all out. Is there something we could learn to make our relationships work?

Let's take a look at some of the issues on both sides to see if there aren't reasonable answers to reasonable questions being asked by men and women. I can say up front that while the complaints are legitimate, the responses come in large part from developing increased awareness and sensitivity toward our differences so that we can put down our weapons and declare peace.

"So, what do you *Do?*"

One of the questions we often hear from men is why women care so much about what they do for a living. No matter what reason women may have for asking, men clearly hear this question as: "how much money do you make?" It is a question whose answer reveals not only wealth but status. Men just don't want to be eliminated on the basis of how much money they make.

Does this mean that women are in search of the ultimate sugar daddy, or one who can support them in a fashion to which they would like to become accustomed? Are women lazy or simply practical? And what ever happened to the notion of equality?

Women may as well know that men have a fair amount of anxiety about this. They wonder, What is the *real* deal? Does his work make the difference in whether or not a woman decides to date him? And if so, why should he even consider taking her out, based on that shallow pre-requisite?

What does their profession or line of work have to do with love and romance potential, anyway? Is it really possible to feel *more* for a person because of their career status or the amount of money they make? Perhaps women aren't so concerned about romance, only about cutting to the chase for marriage potential. We can't marry someone who cannot support a family. But can "marriage potential" *exclude* romance and/or love?

Some men think women secretly believe that a guy with money is more lovable and even if he proves not to be, the relationship is more bearable when you have the easy life of financial security. And who could deny that money does facilitate life, to some extent. Since one of the reasons why people break up relates to money issues, then we can only guess that at least this is one less thing we have to be concerned with, should we marry into money. But we also acknowledge that the notion that money makes a man more lovable or bearable is likely not the case.

What the male population probably could know is that men with money generally display a confidence that is attractive to women. Since self worth is often a function of what one achieves, a man with money and position has likely accomplished a great deal and feels good about himself. It's well known that when we feel good about ourselves we project ourselves in such a way as will attract others who feel good about themselves and us.

Money *IS* power, after all. And power, we all recognize, can be pretty sexy. Even Henry Kissinger was once quoted saying, "Power is the great aphrodisiac."

Nevertheless, money can give us a false sense of confidence because it is measured in terms of the outside world, what society holds up as worthy. If one does not possess an "internal" self-worth, the surface kind will not sustain them. In other words, sooner or later, they will be "found out."

But the genders should be closer than they ever were before as the disparity between the sexes has lessened somewhat in the money arena. We ought to have more in common then ever before, with greater numbers of women in the workforce. Couples can share the experience of the balancing act that occurs between a work life and a home life. It would seem that both genders would be curious about what the other does for a living, as it gives cues to compatibility and common interests, enabling us to define lifestyle. Still, we know that despite the progress made on behalf of the women's movement, there continues to be some struggle for economic parity. This may help explain why women want their male partners to earn at least what they do and meet the standards that they themselves have achieved.

Men shouldn't be put off by this kind of inquiry, as women are more seeking an equal partner than a sugar daddy. And I believe most men probably like that idea a whole lot more than some of us would think. In every aspect of being a couple or raising a family, it would seem that the sexes today are able to do a good deal more sharing *within* responsibilities than their parents may have.

We are probably dealing with residual feelings left over from historical stereotypes that created expectations we tried desperately to live up to. Just as women had been given the message that their looks are *far too* important, men were *supposed* to be able to "take care" of their woman and family someday. That's at least part of the reason behind the numbers of women with eating disorders, literally killing themselves to look good, and why so many men feel challenged, perhaps intimidated by a question that defines their monetary worth. Both men and women continue to suffer from sensitive egos that have everything to do with society's definitions.

Certainly we possess the intellectual understanding: We all know that we are more than a face and body and that true worth has nothing to do with a bank account. One would think so. Still, is our intellectual acknowledgement enough to preclude our strong emotions from leading us in other directions and tell a different story? Not if we continue to be bothered by how good-looking we are and how much money we have.

Perhaps by the time we are in our thirties we have had enough experiences, and we are more mature about some of this stuff. It doesn't bother us so much that we aren't as beautiful as someone else or as thin, or as rich. Perhaps by then, we wouldn't allow the superficial to stand in our way of meeting new people; we are not as self-conscious. This will happen, but only if we have the self-acceptance that necessarily precedes this change in our thinking. Self-acceptance is exciting and attractive. It looks good on us, and we will project the confidence that it brings. Confidence is the necessary ingredient that propels us to take action against being lonely and alone. And it draws people to us because they like who we are.

It is not certain that achievements made in the direction of equality between the sexes will meet with everyone's satisfaction. We would be better to celebrate our differences rather than making an issue with the fight to be similar. We need to come to terms with the fact that men and women are equal, but not the same. Instead of endless and futile battles, the so-called gender war could be ended right here --in the celebration. We have the power to change, to choose different responses. And to come to viable compromises. By virtue of the fact that it is our thinking that needs to change, it is not a cosmetic surface kind of change. It takes a conscious commitment to a change in our beliefs in order to see it and feel it in our lives.

Building relationships could never be done using our differences as weapons, anyway. Accepting, instead, and learning to live within the framework of the value that our differences bring, is the only way to resolution on this.

The focus in dating and relationship building has to be more of a give instead of a get mentality. When we are busy with thoughts of getting, it sounds like we're not sure there is enough, that we may not get what we need if we don't fight for it. It is coming from a fear of scarcity rather than a desire for abundance. Such fear-based thinking can never come from the heart; it can only generate more fears and prevent communication. Instead, if we come from a desire to give something of ourselves, we open the door to receiving, as people are easily drawn toward us and wish to give back to us.

Issues of looks and income levels will inevitably be somewhere present in our relationships with one another for our lives. Someone is always going to make more money than we do and live a more relaxed and privileged lifestyle. At the same time, someone will always be better looking than we are. If this is troublesome for us, this may be an insecurity that needs to be addressed prior to becoming involved with anyone.

When we strip away the facades of these and many other stereotypes, we get to what the real problem is – often, it is a sign of a diminished self-esteem. In a subconscious search for an ego extension, we need to convince others that we are 'good enough' to have the attachment of wealth, status or a fine looking partner by our side. When people see what we *have*, they'll *know* we are something!

We all know that ultimately, the person who seeks only good looks in a person eventually ends up disappointed. When we soon discover that the looks are not enough to sustain our interest, we feel let down. The expectation is left unfulfilled: They *are* beautiful, we *should be* thrilled, happy, fulfilled. Unless we are really attracted to an individual heart and soul, however, the body will only prove temporarily interesting.

Likewise, one seeking *only* wealth in a partner will inevitably be faced with their own feelings of lack, which caused them to make such a mistake. Money is a diversion. If we *need* money, our belief has to be very attached to this temporal world. We may think that it is our ticket to happiness, when in reality it can be the quickest, surest way to divert our attention from what is truly meaningful in our lives. We will learn, as have many before us, that money could never buy us true love or happiness.

Finally, we cannot look for a date or prospective life partner to make us happy, no matter how good-looking or rich they are. Whenever we rely on a source *outside* ourselves and exclude our internal voice, we will not only choose wrongly, we will always be disappointed. No one can do for us what we only can do for ourselves. We need to be happy first, before we go out there and even begin to date people.

What Men could Know about Women

There have been numerous times when I am personally struck by the despair of women about men, but also about how men fail to understand women…they don't get it, what does a woman really want?

Dr. Joyce Brothers mentions nine things women should tell the men they love. Some of them may surprise us:

1. Women need genuine, personal displays of affection
2. Few women really think they are beautiful, or beautiful enough

3. Women are serious about work
4. Women need a sympathetic ear
5. Women don't fall in love as easily as men do
6. Women are good problem solvers
7. Sometimes a woman has to be alone
8. Romance begins in the kitchen
9. A woman wants to be friends with her husband

In addition, it is clear to me that women, as well as men, need appreciation and to be listened to. They need to feel that they matter, that they are important to someone. And they need to feel safe within the relationship.

What Women could Know about Men

1. A man needs for a woman to make him feel strong, capable, intelligent, knowledgeable, and sexy.
2. A man wants and needs to be accepted as he is, not as a woman wants and needs him to be.
3. A man usually wants the woman to understand and be interested in what he does so he can discuss things of importance to him at work.
4. Men like to be complimented on physical attributes as much as women do, so let him know (only if sincere) what it is that you appreciate about his masculinity.
5. Appreciation and admiration for things he does, says, and what he stands for will make him feel important, like he makes a difference.
6. What women do most wrong is to say and do things that are often

emasculating. Women need to help *reassure* men of their masculinity.

7. A man's sexuality is important to his self-image; he may need to feel desired to feel good about himself.
8. Oftentimes, men feel that love and self-worth are demonstrated through sex.

On Sex, (According to Alexandra Penny, *How To Keep Your Man Monogamous, 1989*):

1. Women need to make and take time to make love. They need to stop putting so many other things first and not think of sex as a obligation to be squeezed in.
2. Women need to be involved in the sex. They should not *always* expect the man to take the lead.
3. Using the term of "sexual surrender," Penny writes about the necessity for a woman to fill a man's ego need for conquest and power. He wants to feel that the woman is absolutely abandoning herself to the pleasures of the moment with him.
4. A woman who is aware of and empathizes with a man's sexual functioning will be a good lover. Women need to make an effort to understand man's performance anxiety.
5. Men sometimes enjoy sex with love, but other times can enjoy sex for the pure physical enjoyment.
6. Women need to believe that sex doesn't have to get boring. Penny says that a satisfying monogamous sexual relationship is possible, but only if the couple believes it.

Sex is important to men, probably more important than it is to women, as we have read and heard time and again. If we add that to the fact that they are more visual than women are, then we understand that we do indeed come from different perspectives. Women need to acknowledge this so that when they are in a relationship, they can be sensitive to the man's needs and honest about their own.

The Hunter/ Gatherer Instinct

Primitive man was by necessity a hunter. Those hunting instincts make him by nature very different from his female partner. He wants the challenge, but not too much of one. He focuses on one goal at a time, which sometimes means that once he gets the woman, it's no longer a challenge or a goal. Translated by women, this means we fight for his attention, wondering what ever happened? It's easy to understand how a woman would miss being the target of her man's desires.

Women, we are told, are more like gatherers, causing them to wander and discover. Having a relationship to them doesn't mean it's time to relax, it means it's time to reveal and uncover and unearth, disclose. Translated by men, this means women talk too much, they want to know too much; their demands for intimacy are overwhelming.

A man's identity is said to be tied in to what he does for a living or achievement, and sex, while a woman's needs are more about intimacy and loving. Men speak to make a point, while women share. Women value conversation, they connect to others in that way, and meet their needs for intimacy through sharing personal information. Men value their independence and distance, even as they see themselves as part of a team. A woman sees this distance and independence need as a hindrance to intimacy.

Of course, we have evolved from our primitive roots. But this does help explain why dating for most men may be a bit different than for most women. Men don't mind the hunt. While they are engaged in it, they know what they have to do to get what they want and need. Once they achieve their goal, it becomes a utilitarian exercise. Like so much else, winning a woman is a game of logic. It's challenge, competition for survival, independence, and control. If it doesn't work this time, it's on to the next.

Women are very involved with how it feels, and effects others—more of a cooperative spirit. When we discussed the gender bias in the construct of the psychological assessments, this is one of the common differences exhibited by the sexes. The "left-brain" characteristic is maculine, meaning a stronger propensity for task-orientation, objectivity, and concrete thinking. The tendency to be more global in thinking, abstract, and subjective is associated with a feminine characteristic. The female "right-brain" bent may reveal the gathering instinct of their feminine ancestors. From a dating perspective, this can mean that they need more time and information to process, approaching more deliberately with emotion and intuition. They are trying to take it all in, assimilate and understand everything.

If it weren't for the orientation issues tripping us up, it would seem we are perfectly well matched. While men tend to negotiate, women cooperate. Men still protect, women nurture. Women may analyze a problem, while a man's primary focus is to solve it. Between these things and personality differences, there really is a great deal of potential for balance in a love relationship.

Our evolution has been interesting, and although our recent history is changing us somewhat, traditional beliefs still prevail to a larger degree than we would tend to think. Women are becoming more independent in their financial, social, and even sexual roles. There are many experts who believe that women are becoming so much more like men, with the good news that they are stronger and capable of caring for themselves. The bad news is that they are becoming subject to the same stresses of the traditional male world. With women no longer looking for the financial security need to be fulfilled by her man, she is free to select someone who can provide emotional closeness. Still, there is enough evidence that women continue to have certain expectations of men and men continue to have certain expectations of women. As Susan Jeffers wrote in *Opening Our Hearts To Men (1989)*, this is because

Unreasonable expectations are the basis of so much of (women's) disappointment in our relationships with men and our relationships with ourselves. It is also the basis of so much of our anger. (p74)

Dr. Jeffers credits the confusion to mixed messages women send men. She agrees with other experts who suggest that what women say and what they want are often different, making their true beliefs suspect.

Some men are confused for more reasons other than what women say they want and what they seem to want. As boys, they were taught to hold back their emotions, not to talk about their feelings. Now they are being asked to step out of that comfort zone to listen to and participate in personal discussions about feelings. They have traditionally demonstrated their love and intimacy through sex, in being a good provider for their family, and by taking charge of the "manly" things in operating a household. That's how they felt useful and needed and rewarded. But today, love is more likely to be defined from a woman's point of view—it's about discussion, talking openly, and being intimate through a personal discussion of feelings. That level of sharing is not always natural to many men. It is out of his comfort zone. If therapy comes in to play, another female institution, it requires intimate discussion of what is personal and private. Can men comply with these demands that are still somewhat foreign to their natures, even if and when they are motivated?

By now, if we are like most people looking for answers to the dating game, we are tired of hearing how man and woman are from two separate cultures, speak different languages, even originate from two different planets. Here we not only confirm all this but also perhaps add a few other points of differences to consider between the sexes. Women are learning to detach, while men are learning to connect; each must move toward the center. Nonetheless, not one of us who studies or reports these differences does so with a message of futility. On the contrary, it is in hopes of making a contribution toward understanding our differences. Understanding, that leads to acceptance. It is intended to lower our defenses about our gender differences that undoubtedly persist, and offer solutions to communication despite those differences.

I found what I think is a good summary of the gender differences according to Ellen Kreidman, author of *Light His Fire/Light Her Fire (1995)*:

A woman goes through life with her heart.
A man goes through life with his head.

A man says "I think," which is the logical response.
A woman says "I feel," the emotional response.

A man sees the whole or the overview.
A woman sees the details.

A man says, "In general, what happened?"
A woman says, "Tell me exactly, word for word, what happened?"

A man works on goals.
A woman works on relationships.

A man says, "I need to feel good about what I do."
A woman says, "I need to feel good about who we are."

A man needs little or no preparation for sex.
A woman needs hours of emotional and mental preparation.

A man is stimulated by sight.
A woman is stimulated by words.

"Desperate" to Marry

In a bygone era, it certainly was acceptable and even expected that a woman marry in her late teens, early twenties. Men have never really had age limitations imposed on them from societal expectations, so they married whenever. For the most part, men continue to enjoy this kind of freedom from social expectations and restrictions.

Today, while it is acceptable to wait to marry with a greater percentage of females in career positions, it looks as if this idea works well until about the mid-30s age range. After that, biology takes over for women, but men around this age are likewise concerned that they will never meet the "right one," they will never marry. Men's doubts about children have more to do with the waning desires and physical limitations of an "older father."

The woman's obvious biological concern often leaves her wide open and forces her to weigh alternatives. These may be alternatives many men never even have to consider. We might think it is a vengeful God who has thrust this limitation upon the female gender, {If it hadn't been for that first lady in the garden...}.

I do not think that this is the case at all, however. Perhaps it simply demonstrates the critical importance of the female nurturer's role. The matter today is mitigated by scientific developments that have made it possible for women to give birth well into their 40s. It isn't even necessary for a woman to have a man in her life, because she can use a sperm bank. All these advancements ought to level the playing field for women and lessen their pressing concerns about marrying by a certain age.

Despite such advancements, however, we all think and develop our separate philosophies. I have spoken to people who are adamant in their belief that anytime after their 20s is too late to have children, and so they are pursuing marriage with a vengeance. Others are perfectly comfortable waiting until their 30sand 40s, pointing to greater maturity and readiness for such a huge responsibility and change in their lives. It is, after all, an individual choice based on our unique perceptions about the way things ought to be.

Knowing this about ourselves is smart as it is important to have similar values and goals as your life partner. Most importantly, we must accept and trust that at each moment every one of us is precisely where we need to be. When we relax, stop trying to control outcomes, things do magically fall into their rightful place.

The 5 most horrible misperceptions we can have about a partner:

1. **I can fix him; He'll be fine or she'll change** ONCE WE get married!

Here's what we must all understand: Whatever our partner is today, he or she will only be more of that tomorrow. We must not marry people with the idea that we are going to -- or that we even *can* - - change them. This simply is not ever the case. We are neither that powerful nor is it our right to change *anyone*. Do yourself and your date a favor and don't even go out for a second time if this is a thought that occurs to you on the FIRST!

From Frog to FAIRYTALE...

...So you thought that you could date someone...and turn him/her into a prince...or princess...??

WRONG!!!! What do you think you are ... a magician?

If we date, or even think of a serious relationship, with a single thought of changing anyone, we are surely making one of the biggest mistakes of our life. We will get no one to change, and worse, we will grow to dislike the person, have regrets and feel resentment.

First, I say don't do this. At the very least, don't believe that it is even possible to change anyone. Then, if we really care and wish to learn, we need to find out why we are inclined to select people who we have a desire to change in the first place. I mean, why wouldn't we simply meet people who we thought were great just the way they are? Is it because we have something going on that we need to address in *ourselves*?

Sometimes, when we see faults in others, particularly if we keep seeing the *same* problems in a number of others, it is because we are looking in the mirror and see something wrong with ourselves. It is much easier to point the finger of blame at someone else, as they become our targets for our secret self-reproach.

In the book, *How To Make Love All The Time*, author Barbara DeAngelis, Ph.D., discusses how we cannot expect to attract a certain type of person when we do not exhibit the same type of attributes we expect of them. She also warns us not to be looking at someone for "their potential," but for one who is already "becoming the person we want to be with, someone who is interested in growing in that direction."

2. **Afraid of the "C" WORD...**

Some people do not appear to want to commit. They may feel too young, too busy, too immature, or too lazy. They are not ready and as an old line explains "A man convinced against his will, is of the same opinion still." We are all better off not pushing it.

Of course, no one's afraid of a word, they are afraid of what the word might *mean*... It may conjure up unpleasant memories for some, spell imminent disaster for others because of past experiences and preconceived thoughts on the subject. Perhaps they've seen one two many divorces -- Mean, ugly divorces. The thought 'That's not happening to me' takes over the person, perhaps over-sensitizing them to the downside of the committed life. These are distorted perceptions. Each situation is new and unique, not to be judged by another. People who judge the present through the wounded eyes of the past are hurt. We mustn't judge them harshly as they have already been hard on themselves. If we love them, we are patient; we remain a teacher and positive role model. No, they aren't afraid of the word, they are terrified because they do not know *how to do what the word means.*

When we say *commitment,* it has to do with a state of monogamy, continuity, or consistency and longevity. That means that we expect our partner to be loyal, reliable, and to be with us for as long as they can or perhaps want to. Of course, in traditional marriage terms, we expect a forever commitment. Most of us recognize that if something changes to affect that aspect of the union, we will be involved in an abbreviated contract.

It's one thing to commence a serious relationship with all good intentions to have this commitment be a shared and purposeful permanent situation. But, some actually start out ignoring a gut message, opting instead to "give it a try." If it doesn't work out, well, there's always breakup and divorce. Divorce, especially in the U.S., is made far too readily available, with 1.2 million divorces granted in each of the past three years. This was the likely rationale behind the one-year legal separation requirement in divorces with no urgent grounds.

But even in a serious monogamous committed relationship, why would we want to invest that much time and energy, only to end up apart? Think about the word "try." It is a misnomer. We either will or we won't; we do or we don't. There is no such thing as *trying* to make a relationship work. We may hide behind it, but we are predicting our failure when we use this language--even if only to ourselves. Try to turn the page of this book. What happens? You either turn it or you don't; *trying* is irrelevant, isn't it?

People who use a tentative approach to serious commitment are no more useful to the idea of a long-term relationship than those who strictly do not commit. In fact, they are *least* useful to the concept of a commitment, as they are less truthful than those who admit that they are not ready. When we've got one foot in the relationship and the other one ready to exit, it is doomed from the start. This is not a game that we play at. This is life, ours and another's, with both families usually involved and active copartners. If we feel somehow that we may as well do this for now, while still secretly waiting for a "better offer," we should slap our cheek, wake ourselves up and pray hard that we change our thinking. We ought to ask for help; we need it bad.

There are some of us who do not have a very clear idea of how to have a relationship that is monogamous. This may be a function of what we have been exposed to --partly nature and part environment, as we know so many characteristics are. It's okay to love a person like that, but eventually when it comes time to be serious, we will need to do some soul searching. Either we stay, knowing what we will face, attempting to get agreement on the counseling it may take for our partner to agree on the value of monogamy, or we will decide that we are unable to work that out. (Remember, it's not the love that has to go, it's the relationship.) Monogamy cannot be compromised inside the context of a traditional committed relationship.

Another reason that some people are unable to commit to monogamous relationships is due to honesty. When we know that we are unable to do it, we refuse to enter the institution of marriage because we know that we will be unfaithful. Rather than enter and cheat anyway, we just say no prior to the legal entanglement. Now that makes these folks sound oddly ethical because rarely do we call it "cheating" when there is no commitment.

It turns out that infidelity itself may be scientifically explainable. In an emerging field called evolutionary psychology, evidence suggests that there is, in fact, a correlation between families that tend to be monogamous and those that tend not to be. Scientists claim it has more to do with a pattern of giving in to natural impulses versus repressing those same natural desires. The thing to understand is that whatever our decision, it will have been our choice. So when we select our individual response, we are accountable for that choice and can blame no one. We have only to take responsibility for our decision, whether or not it can be understood.

3. **Looks are the Number One thing**

Again, the perception is that most, if not all of us, are interested in good looks. To people who feel that if someone is not packaged just right there is no use even speaking to them ... let us say, shame, shame. It is their loss. Forget the beauty is only skin deep routine. Simply consider all the beautiful people we miss out on if we are so focused on a "certain look."

It's a good thing that each of us has unique definitions for what we call good looks, anyway. Part of the chemistry thing has to do with the way someone looks to us, that's sure. And chemistry is an important element in sustaining our attraction to someone. But it's not the number one thing we love about a partner. Or at least it shouldn't be.

Our reliance on looks may be put to the test with the newer dating vehicles like voice personals. Speaking to someone over the phone without the intrusion of our physical appearance can in a way offer a good advantage to those of us who do not consider ourselves particularly good-looking. We have an opportunity to shine and for someone to get to know us before they are even able to judge our looks and whether we are their physical "type."

4. **Men NEED sex**

This is absolute, complete nonsense! No one, male or female, *needs* sex! We like sex, we *want* sex, but never, ever, do we need it. Using Webster's noun definition of the word, it is neither a necessity nor obligation; it is not a "compulsion" either, although some may wish to argue this point.

When a guy tries to convince a woman about sex against her better judgment, she should turn around and walk away. She can't win. If she engages in sex with him because she *believes* he needs it, she will be miserable afterward, and devastated when he doesn't call. If she has sex because she too wants it, things could get real ugly because it probably means that she has already developed some attachment to this man. In the unfortunate event that he does not share in that feeling, she *will* be hurt. She is better not to pursue the physical relationship as her bond will intensify after the "lovemaking," while his may not.

If a woman wants a man for sex, it may be a compliment, but unless it's mutual, and unless it could develop into something more, a man generally loses interest. A relationship like this gets less interesting to a man as he matures.

It is true that many more men view sex as a physical performance and release than do women. They are more likely than women to have sex without emotional attachment, at least in their youth. Women tend to be immediately emotional about the experience. Either way, though, none of us needs waste love on one-night stands who have no intention to reciprocate.

5. **Sexual satisfaction is difficult for a woman**

It would seem that there wouldn't be too much for women to know about satisfying a man. If we are to judge by the end "goal," it appears that it is accomplished rather easily. But this isn't an accurate statement, it's just that we hear more from women who talk about how little men know about satisfying their partners. Complaints from males generally amount to the lack of interest demonstrated by their female partners. This was most common among those who had been married awhile, but the genders are probably a lot closer on this issue than we tend to believe.

It is true that women are built differently than are men, that there are a few more intricate details to know about how and what a woman responds to. But the truth is that in general, and with some obvious exceptions, the sex act has a very difficult time separating itself from the emotional bond between two people. And the satisfaction part has more to do with how much the one partner wants to please the other. It's such a natural act that we probably don't need lessons so much as patience. We need to reserve our physical expression of love for those with whom we share an emotional closeness. There would probably be far fewer complaints, if that were the case.

For those of us who believe that sex is a skill that can indeed be taught, I might suggest that the thought of it as a skill is somewhat disappointing. I am sure that we can learn as we go along, but it is so much a heart and soul matter, is it not? The knowledge gained by treating it as a skill may be rendered useless as it will prove to be temporary window-dressing, lacking the kind of change that will be necessary to sustain it.

Sex was never intended to be mechanical, more an ultimate expression of love. When I speak to people about teaching their partner, they wince, say it is not particularly appealing to have to *teach* someone. Doesn't that kind of take the fun, much less excitement, out of it? We do want our partners to think of something on their own, and do it, rather than simply going through motions. We all know the difference, and usually it is manifest in our responses to our partner. If we sense the other person isn't as interested as we are, there is a palpable change in our attitude towards it and behavior following it.

Most men do want to know what their female partner wants and needs, particularly in the bedroom. Women should really make an effort here because they may be very pleasantly surprised by the outcome. Just don't make a huge deal of it. Women should neither feel self-conscious about such expression, nor should they assume that they are being presumptuous or insulting to men. It is important to men to know what a woman wants, and it isn't fair to expect him to guess or to be judged when he guesses wrong.

Why *isn't* so called "chemistry" enough? Isn't it supposed to kind of *take care of everything*-- when it comes to sexual response, it just happens in the context of the passionate attraction?? No one has to tell anyone what to do; it's just there, naturally, right? Perhaps that is one logical conclusion, but this is probably easier at the beginning of a relationship rather than throughout the course of a long lasting one. Since chemistry is part physiological, there may need to be a conscious effort to sustain it long-term.

No matter which way you examine the issue, however, both men and women can be a little more patient and a lot more creative. Most of the good part in lovemaking happens having *nothing* to do with any particular body part, exclusively. Two people need to trust the chemistry to lead them in the direction of fulfillment for both, remaining open, secure, and communicative about the possibilities.

I cannot help but think of a Chico Marx quote:

"I wasn't kissing her, I was whispering in her mouth." Okay, maybe he was trying to be funny, but when I first read that, I considered how sexy the whisper would be. The *idea* is usually sexier than the act. It is about taking time, there is no need to hurry through anything. What are we rushing for? As we all probably know, taking that extra time makes it so much more pleasurable.

If we are not likely to ask or to tell our partner, perhaps even resent having to spoon feed him or her, we needn't be concerned. There are many people who do very well at lovemaking who haven't been taught, they haven't had to view dirty pictures or movies in preparation, and they haven't even had to ask, "What would you like me to do, honey?" They simply do what comes natural, and get to know through trial and error what their partner responds to. There is something to be said for pushing aside our inhibitions and just doing what comes naturally. We may be making much more of it than we need to. Our natural instincts, particularly when we love deeply and are paying attention, will guide us and never let us down.

The one characteristic that allows us to be naturally good lovers is when we are focused on giving or pleasing our partner. Mutual satisfaction, not physical performance, is the intent. Good "performance" is probably a by-product of the desire to please.

In an effort to dispel the myth, women *can* be as satisfied as men are with the sexual experience. A woman is fully capable of achieving complete and total satisfaction, just as a man does. If you are a woman and either still do not know this or have bought into some bogus notion about how sex is more about a man than a woman, stop now and replace that erroneous information in your mind with what you probably suspected all along anyway. If you are a man and don't yet know or are guilty of perpetuating such silly and false notions, shame on you. You might want to try making love in a way that is mutually satisfying. I'll wager you'll like that much better.

Some say that when it comes to the physical component of love, we may be better to keep the mystery alive by doing, not by talking about it, anyway. Reducing sex down to the level of discussion makes it just another relationship "issue" (especially for most men). This isn't light "pillow talk," but perhaps the too serious "Let's discuss this" kind of conversation. That intimidates most of us, anyway. It can make us feel like we don't know something, and that someone else *has taught our partner* and that he or she *did that* with someone else, and it will go on and on and on...! It's back to that sensitive ego thing again. And we know when we get caught up in that web, no one quite finds an easy way out.

Fidelity

Interestingly enough, men and women also differ in their responses to infidelity. Studies in evolutionary psychology have confirmed that a man has greater difficulty with sexual infidelity than emotional infidelity. Women are just the opposite. To women, the real threat exists in redirected love and attachment, not in "supplementary sex." For men, it is the physical act that causes him greater distress. (Time, August 15, 1994,

"Our Cheating Hearts" by Robert Wright.) No surprise there.

Another study quoted in the same article revealed that single men with higher income, education, and job status had the "busiest sex lives" (based on frequency and the number of partners). No surprise there, either.

Does that suggest, perhaps if only on a subconscious level, that men who seek power and wealth are more apt to rely on that in order to attract the opposite sex? So, following this out to at least one possible logical conclusion, these men are *not* those who possess a great *inner* self worth -- that they are somewhat *dependent* on external allure to attract their women? I don't believe this and neither should you. As the article put it, "It is only natural that the exquisitely flexible human mind should be designed to capitalize on power once it is obtained." Interesting word, *capitalize...*

The article rightly concludes that we have one of two choices. Although we may all have, at one time or another, interest in a sexual partner *other* than the one to whom we are committed, we can either act on it or we can choose to inhibit those impulses for the sake of the relationship. Giving in to such "natural" impulses would be considered insensitive to our beloved partner, almost barbaric and irresponsible. On the other hand, the idea of holding back, while in some way sounds repressive, is both considerate and respectful. It would appear to be the responsible and mature decision. Experts in the field of evolutionary psychology, about whom the author writes, would call it the "moral" choice.

♥ ♥ ♥

DateNotes

- Our gender differences are inevitable and somewhat legendary. We keep fighting to understand one another, having been engaged in this battle for centuries. Perhaps it is better if we simply accept one another, because the more we try to under stand, the more frustrated it seems we get, and the more it causes feelings of wanting to change the other person. Whenever any of us feels that someone wants us to change, we dig in our heels to resist. Since this cannot be unconditional love, we are probably better off without it, anyway.

- I believe men when they tell me that money is very important to a woman, as I believe woman who say that looks are too important to a man. And although I want to suggest that we should accept this, I am tempted to warn not to let this get in the way of dating and approaching anyone you want to. Being rejected never killed anyone, and remember the adage about having nothing to lose. It is all in the way you look at it. If "losing" to you is hearing the word no, then you are in trouble. But you cannot lose what you never had, so why not first see if it is possible to have it? You might be pleasantly surprised!

- It doesn't ever hurt to keep educating yourself on the opposite sex. It undoubtedly raises our sensitivity and causes us to become conscious about some of our behavior that may get in the way of a good relationship. The knowledge you gain and the subsequent action or change that is inevitable will never go unappreciated.

♥ Some of the value in understanding our primitive roots and what we can glean out of evolutionary psychology has a way of relaxing our fears about not being cared for. We are better able to depersonalize offenses and allow the other person to not feel judged. When we don't feel judged, we are free to act in more loving ways. Everyone gets to benefit from complete unconditional acceptance.

♥ We have also lived with our many misperceptions as they stubbornly resist change because we haven't changed our thinking about it. The five I have attempted to correct:

1. We can't change anyone
2. Fear of commitment is a disguise
3. Looks aren't number one in the grand scheme of things
4. No one ever died from a lack of sex and
5. Women can not only enjoy sex, but can experience sexual satisfaction, are only the major ones I found to be repeated within a two year period of talking to people.

There are obviously many more of these myths. We need to be aware of these and others and abandon such thinking in favor of more productive thoughts.

- Infidelity is hurtful, whether it is viewed from a male or female point of view. If you are tempted to be with someone else, it probably says something negative about the relationship you are in. If you do not have the courage to discuss it and work it out with your mate, then don't solve it by going out and hurting more people than need to be hurt. This is when empathy would work well in directing you to a better solution. You could eliminate feelings of guilt and afford the someone you are with the greatest dignity while maintaining your own sense of integrity. If you still choose to leave in the end, you will have made that decsion in a way for everyone to feel as positive as they can under the circumstances.

Six

THE "EX-FACTOR"

It is secular as well as spiritual wisdom to beware of divorce. If you do not come to deeply understand and fully accept your own personal responsibility for "irreconcilable differences" in marriage number one, it is quite possible you will discover the very same sort of insoluble problems in marriage number two.

M. Scott Peck, M.D..
A World Waiting To Be Born (p136)

We all know that there is a difference between being in the dating scene very early on, still in our 20s, and being in it for the second and third time around. The difference isn't only about age, of course; there is a host of other differences that have come about due to experience and the knowledge gained. There may be children. All these differences cause us to be in a different place, have perhaps different attitudes, objectives, and concerns about dating. Let's address some of the major ones.

Jane is a divorced women with two young children, ages 8 and 10. She admits that she is definitely interested in seeing men, but she isn't necessarily interested in "dating." When I asked her to elaborate, she said that her interest in going out with someone is limited to whether or not there is something that could be developed into a "serious relationship." She determines this potential within the first one or two dates, and then either makes it clear that she is interested, or sends them on their way. In speaking to Jane, one gets the distinct impression that she has no time to play games or "waste time." She would rather break off sooner than later with someone, and has no qualms about letting him know.

While it is completely understandable for a woman to be straightforward about her intentions, Jane could be premature in her determination and possibly scare off someone who may be interested but needs more time. If there is no chemistry, then it's one thing. But if there is, and she breaks it off because she perceives he is too slow in coming up with the "right" answers and approach, then she could cheat herself out of a very positive experience, possibly long-term relationship.

Jane was representative of the women I had spoken to who had been divorced and had young children. "Dating" appeared to be an activity they had joyfully engaged in before they were married, but now somehow it seemed an unwelcome intrusion in their very busy lives. They like men, they want to be re-married, but they have different thoughts about what it will take to get them to respond to someone. They had learned a thing or two, and it appeared they wanted to benefit from their experience in as many ways as they possibly could. Many of them were focused on their children and concerned about getting involved with someone the least bit questionable. They felt they needed to assess things relatively quickly in order to decide whether they would bother introducing the children. Some spoke about the attachment/detachment drama that children are often subjected to when a single parent decides to bring someone in to the home. It wasn't worth it, in their estimation.

This scenario appeared to be consistent with the descriptions in *Finding Love, Creative strategies for finding your ideal mate*, by Drs. Margaret O' Connor and Jane Silverman (1989). They write that the "older crowd," who they identify to be the primary users of personals ads, tend to be candid, attend to detail, serious about wanting to find someone, and willing to accept less than perfection (p 91).

Women who had grown children or children in mid-to-late teens were slightly different. They didn't seem to have the same kind of concerns with the children. Most of these women described their lives after divorce as much happier than in their marriages. They were hesitant to "get serious" right away, expressing an interest in dating, but perhaps with one man, as soon as they could possibly get there. These women spoke of the new-found freedom they cherished, with everything from not having to cook to being able to sleep in the middle of their beds. They also had developed many friendships with other women, which fulfilled the need to have someone to do things with, and found it less important to have a man for that purpose.

One man, I'll call Ed, considered himself a virtual expert in the "dating game." He was twice divorced, two grown children only with his first wife, and around mid-to-late 40s. He mostly dated women in their 30s and made it a point to find out early in their communication whether they were looking to have children. Since he would not be interested in another family, he cleared the air before anything serious could be developed.

Ed decided about 10 years ago, after his first divorce, that he needed to get assertive about the prospect of dating. With his busy schedule, often out of town on business and a variety of other social activities and regular work out routine, he chose the newspaper to advertise what he was looking for in a mate. When he suggested that he thought of it as being a lot like looking for a job, that traditional ways simply weren't enough, especially for someone in his position, I simply smiled. He explained that he has met a number of very nice professional women, one of whom he lived with for two years, and a few others he dated for a fair amount of time. Incidentally, Ed was not at all apologetic about his interest in looks, reinforcing most everything I had read and heard about that priority for men. The next two characteristics he sought were a sense of humor and personality.

One would think that Ed would have good reason to be cautious and hesitant, I suppose, since he was twice divorced by women who decided to leave him for another man. In fact, his last wife specifically told him that she was interested in the other man because of what he could provide financially. She did subsequently marry that man, who had also been cheating on his wife with her. In addition, Ed has had negative experiences beyond those two. But, he was not bitter or angry at women, instead his was upbeat, optimistic, and certain that the individual who ends up with him will be a lucky woman. I couldn't disagree.

I learned that Ed had a great deal of information about using the voice personals service that might be helpful to mention here. He views the advancement to voice versus letter-writing to be a distinct advantage and definite improvement in convenience to its users. He finds that in addition to the content of the message, it is particularly helpful to hear the person's voice.

Although he writes ads, Ed finds most of his activity comes from responding to ads written by women. He feels that there is a "small window of opportunity," as he referred to it, in which a woman will be available, as she will often receive a multitude of responses. Particularly if she is attractive and "has something going for her," a man has to act fast or lose the opportunity to date her.

As I said, Ed makes it a point not to date women who are interested in a family, but he also avoids ones who have recently broken off from a serious relationship. He defines this period as definitely not before three months has passed, and better if it is 6 months or longer since the break up. And yes, Ed has more screening criteria, which he was happy to share. He has a list of questions that he asks during the first telephone call with the woman. This might offer some good tips for people who feel that they are presently not doing a good enough job of screening, or ones that have no idea what is important to ask before we decide to meet someone. Here are Ed's questions:

- Why did you respond to this ad?
- What are you looking for in a guy?
- Are you over your last relationship?
- How long has it been since your breakup?
- How much time do you like to spend together?
  (once you are dating someone)
- Do you have children? How many? Ages?
- What turns you off about a guy?
- Are you active, a homebody, like to go out? (lifestyle preferences)
- Do you dislike men? Are you a feminist?

Although I did chuckle at a couple of them, I thought most of these questions were fair and straightforward. They were ones that represented the answers Ed needed to make a decision on whether or not he wishes to pursue an individual. We might ask the same, adding or editing to suit our unique needs. Incidentally, I asked about inadequate answers and Ed assured me that he puts his excellent communications skills to work (he is a professional trainer and former teacher) by probing further. He asks good, open-ended questions, such as, "tell me more about that."

There was an interesting point that Ed made related to the number of responses he receives when he places an ad compared to the number of responses he knows women in general receive on their ads. No comparison, he says, as many more men respond to women than woman will respond to men...Which Ed quickly reminds me, "they're telling us they're liberated, but they still want to be pursued!"

Ed and I talked extensively about the statistic revealing that the majority of breakups (said to be as high as 75%) are initiated by women, and about his thoughts on how women handled change better than men did. Theories based on our primitive roots would likely confirm that (due to women's ability to discuss and share emotional problems more readily, making the transition a more smooth and supported one). He discussed how squeamish he is about having been divorced twice, saying that women may be quick to judge someone like him as one who is incapable of making things work. And he talked about how men's egos can easily be shattered, as divorce often means starting over completely financially and emotionally.

Ed also had one more piece of advice to offer. He said that most of us are on our best behavior when we meet someone and we can count on this lasting for 6 months to one year. After that time, he felt that we will get to see who the person really is. In light of our divorce rates, it got me wondering how many people do marry before they "really" know someone.

By its very nature, divorce is never a happy occasion for all involved persons. Even if it is a positive outcome, there are always aspects about it that are difficult and frustrating and cause people to lament, and regret, to get and sometimes remain angry. It is a loss, and as we discussed in our section on the grieving process, it is possible to get stuck in a stage. I found that it might be more a function of the time we feel we invested in good faith, and the betrayal of that "till death" trust.

Lisa had been married for nearly twenty years. She had married when she was only 19. They were the typical struggling young couple, with both trying to finish up college and get jobs. Before she could do that, however, she became pregnant and was forced to put her life on hold. Mike pursued his dream of becoming successfully self-employed. Within five years of marriage, Lisa was a mother of four children, including one set of twins. From her point of view, she was doing all that was expected of her to manage a household while her husband provided financially. Still, with the very busy schedule Lisa had been maintaining, she had barely noticed how that was about all Mike had provided for.

She thought back. She raised the children, as Mike was busy getting on and off planes, going from city to city, to close deals and rub elbows with prominent business contacts. There were times she actually felt sorry for her children, because they hardly saw their dad, and when they did, he could not be available to them. The house was never clean enough, the children never quiet enough, and the sex never often enough. He had stringent standards for Lisa to live up to, and suddenly it became very personal. She was not thin enough, compliant enough, and didn't ever quite look good enough. The more money he made, the more he criticized her spending. Her awareness of their communication problems brought her to a therapist and a request that he join her. When he would not, she saw an attorney.

It took Lisa two years to end the marriage. This had been after many attempts on her part to get Mike to joint counseling and struggling with her own sense of commitment and responsibility to the relationship. Adding insult to injury, within two years of the divorce, Mike sold his company for a multi-million dollar sum. Lisa was excluded from the deal, as their divorce decree had no copy related to her part in the business.

Lisa felt very strongly about how hard she had worked during her marriage. She raised four wonderful children, all of whom Mike proudly claims, and she considered herself a good, dutiful wife. She never felt she got much back from her husband, and now she was virtually nullified with a settlement that failed to recognize her contribution. Lisa felt there was no way that Mike could have been as successful without her, but she would have to settle for a private recognition. Mike would never give her the satisfaction.

Lisa entered the dating scene with caution, but since her self-esteem was somewhat fractured, she forced herself to go out and be reassured that she was indeed attractive. Of course, Lisa found enough people out there to date and with whom she could develop friendships. She said that although she has little interest in marrying again (why should she, she says, there is no reason), she does have an interest in sustaining a long-term relationship. Her life is full without one, however, with a host of friends, her children, and a variety of activities she enjoys. She notes how she can not forget the negative experience of her marriage, because, she says, "if you forget, how do you learn?"

Another woman I know suffered a few indiscretions from her husband before *he* decided to leave *her*. After more than 15 years together, he told her that he "never loved" her. She had great difficulty getting over this because she had taken her vows very seriously. There was never a thought of leaving as she had made the commitment for "better or worse," and even when she was humiliated and completely distraught, she was willing to stay and work things out. Their two sons, nearly adults by the time of the divorce, had equal difficulty with the entire experience, mainly because they were deeply concerned for their mother.

Today this woman is happily with a wonderful man who treated her so well that she hesitated to believe it for some time. She now thanks her ex for allowing her a life that she clearly would not have had because of her willingness to settle.

Men in similar situations after divorce had relatively comparable reactions with the exception of claiming a happier life after divorce (at least immediately). It appeared that this might be linked to the tendency for men to have relied on his spouse for developing social connections with others. When the couple broke up, it was more likely that the woman retained the friendships. This was usually the case unless the original tie had been a function of the man's association.

It is also, men tell me, easier for a woman to be single again. If she is attractive, bright, and smiles at a man, he is likely to ask her out. She has the element of choice, as she is the one who gets asked. Since the man does the asking in most cases, the only choice he usually has is in who he decides to risk rejection from as he is making the decision.

Men also admit that it might be harder for them to get over a relationship break up, especially if their wife was the one to leave. One man explained that if you are in your late 30s, early 40s, going back out there puts you in contact with women who are either in their early 30s or 40s. The women in their early 30s often still want a family, and this is usually not a mutual objective, particularly if the man has had his family already and has no interest in starting that way again. Some women in their 40s already have grandchildren or are looking forward to having them, and being an involved grandparent. That isn't good, either, because this is a guy who enjoys travelling and working out and is involved in lots of activities, especially if his own children are grown.

Mostly, I heard stories of bitterness, resentment, and anger from both men and women. This was true whether the individual was the spouse who left or the spouse who was left. People felt cheated of valuable time. Although this was the case, these were also charming people, who I found to be pleasant, interesting, and very bright. It was clear that they had learned a great deal. But it wasn't always clear that they had learned the most important thing, in my opinion. This had to do with the need to let go, and to accept the end of the relationship as a gift. Without it, these folks could not know themselves quite as well, or what they want in another relationship quite as clearly. At least they should have learned this. Time was a mitigating factor in the negative feelings expressed, but the memories often remained vivid.

Many of the stories like Lisa's reminded me of a similar dynamic operating while I investigated behavior immediately following an involuntary job loss in mid-life professionals. The feelings of betrayal were reminiscent...*I did everything I was supposed to do*.... When we work hard, enter an agreement with commitment and some amount of (usually in the beginning) sacrifice, we expect to get back in return for our hard work and sacrifice. At the very least, we want and need the reassurance that acknowledges our contribution.

Perhaps some of our failed long-term relationships were one-sided, perhaps we weren't paying attention, or maybe we were conscious of the mediocrity but too willing to settle in our complacency or our lack of belief in true happiness. In the end, we would not really choose to be in a relationship that was one-sided and we need to learn that each of us deserves to be happy and fulfilled.

Naturally no one is going to be particularly happy about having to divorce, unless perhaps you were the one to leave and you left because you fell in love with someone else. The people I spoke to who did this were almost apologetic, insisting that their spouse was wonderful, it was them and their needs that led them to another. Still, I felt that theirs was a situation that precluded feelings of bitterness, as they decided to do something about their unhappiness. The only misfortune, I suppose, from a moral perspective, is that they decided to do something about it before they gave a chance to their spouse and at least in one case, before they even disclosed their unhappiness to their spouse. When one person leaves a long-term relationship because of another, my suspicion is that there was an emotional divorce long before it became a physical one. Most therapists and experts seem to agree.

The Opposite of Love

Getting over a love, especially one with whom we were legally entangled, takes courage, strength, and a belief that everything happens for a reason. A good reason. And knowing when you are there is acknowledging not that you "hate" someone, but that you *no longer care.* It is said that the opposite of love is really not hate, but apathy, and this is true. When we get angry, we show that we care and that we still have an investment in what has happened or will happen.

Not caring can sound just as mean as hatred, but I don't think it is, really. What it says is that we no longer have an investment in the outcome of this relationship. Having no investment allows us to jettison negative feelings, and remain optimistic for our new future. The one without the circumstances of our past. Remember, we can still care about the person, it's just that we do not want the relationship.

It's a Verb, Not a Noun…

When I listen to people speak of themselves or their ex-spouse, I often hear how they feel like a "loser," or how their ex is a loser, etc.. What strikes me about this is how often we confuse our nouns with our verbs, and how in the process, we destroy our self-esteem or feel bad that we disparage another (even if we aren't necessarily conscious about why we feel so bad).

The truth is that none of us is a loser, we are all good people who sometimes behave badly. Often we can not even help our actions, because as we already discussed, we are on some automatic pilot that causes us to react, instead of taking the time and proactive thought to respond appropriately. The next time we are tempted toward neurotic self-blaming behavior that compromises our self-esteem, we need to interrupt the tendency to refer to ourselves as "loser" and replace it with the proper verb version: *we lost*...this time.

When we are tempted to refer to another in the same way, because we wish to blame someone, let's correct that reference, too: *they lost*. Sometimes we win, and sometimes we lose and never does that make us worth *less*. It only makes us humans who make mistakes, doing things that are not always in the best of intention for people in our lives, or even for ourselves.

What about the Children?

One of the biggest worries about divorce concerns the children. First, I will address the question that continues to beleaguer parents and that is whether it is (or was) better to stay or leave a marriage that isn't working for the sake of the children. Since that topic surfaced so often in all the conversations I have had with people over time, it seems appropriate to address here, even as this is a chapter about the aftermath of a divorce. And then, we will talk about how to most effectively deal with our children once there is a divorce and we wish to begin dating.

A child will rarely wish his or her parents to part. Unless the home situation is particularly unbearable due to abuse of some kind, most children want their parents to stay together. No one needs me to explain why, it's just the way it is. Once people mature and become adults living outside their parents' home, we will hear "my parents should never have been married." I can not tell you how often I have heard that said. Still, while we are young, our hopes and wishes are for both parents and one home.

It was somewhat surprising to me to learn how many men felt so strongly about this, causing them to stay in unhappy situations long after they would have preferred it to be over, all for the "sake of the children." This sacrifice, which is what it seems like to me, was not necessarily accompanied by infidelity to the spouse. Incidentally, of the men I spoke to, there were an equal number from intact and broken homes.

In general, women felt similarly, but I spoke to a number who disagreed with that perspective. They often spoke about having allowed this for a time, but eventually beginning to think that their children were observing a loveless marriage. Once they were convinced that this was hurtful to their children, they felt likewise convinced about ending the marriage.

As I said, this is a perennial debate, one which will undoubtedly continue with enough examples on both sides to prove its point. What I do know is that children do learn about love from their parents. If that is so, then what do they learn from two people who stay together but do not love each other? Are these the adults who now admit that their parents had no business being married? When I have put this question to people, they usually agree that there is merit in that argument. Still, they continue to believe that there is more benefit to the child in many other ways for parents to fulfill the terms of their contract. Many religions would agree.

Now, about what to do about dating when we still have young children at home—

First, there is no good reason for a single parent to refuse to date simply because they have children. I have heard people say that they choose to wait until their children are grown for many different reasons. Or they can not take the time to do their own "marketing" and subsequent development of a relationship because they are too busy with their children's activities and their work schedules. That is a choice we have, certainly, and if we feel strongly about this, are content and satisfied with our lives the way they are, then there is nothing wrong with that, either. If that is not the case, however, we must question whether or not we are going to learn to resent and blame our children for our unhappiness. That would be far worse for the children than most anything that can happen if you decide to date wisely.

Our children do want us to be happy, just as we want them to be. Once we are ready, we can consider the following points.

Be as open and honest as necessary about your plans to date. If you will be using voice personals, for example, let them know that there may be return phone calls, and how they might take a message, maintaining the privacy you determine is appropriate. Reassure them about what this means. For instance, you won't consider this a replacement for their other parent, etc.

Ask them to be open and honest with you. Both before and after they meet someone you are dating, allow them to express any concerns and respond to them. Usually, they are just afraid of what it means, so try not to be secretive.

Don't introduce your date to your children until you have decided that he or she is someone you care about.

♥ ♥ ♥

DateNotes

- Being single in our 20s without children, is definitely different than being single in our 30s and 40s with children, but we shouldn't make it more than it is. Often the way we think causes us to be in a negative mindset. When we are negative, we set ourselves up for failure. Know that whatever age and circumstances, there are people who are in similar situations, and prospects who not only do not mind your situation, but may like it or be seeking it out for themselves.

- Which brings me to reminding you of vehicles that are available today to meet people. Your job is to find people who are suited to you and your situation. The larger audience you expose your self to, the greater likelihood you will find what you are looking for. Ideal candidates don't come knocking on our door unsolicited anymore than prospective employers come looking for us. We need to take action. Once you make the decision to go forward, do not allow fear to get in your way, even if the fear is so great that it feels like death. Remember that it is always better to die living than it is to live dying.

- If you think of yourself as a loser, then you will look that way to others. We can't help but transmit our feelings. In taking responsibility, it is only necessary that we admit our contribution in the form of the action, not to confuse it with our person. Failure is good as it humbles and instructs us.

- ♥ We might consider how claims of "hate" are more close to caring than we may think and believe. At least it speaks to our investment of feeling toward a person, rather than a complete absence of feeling, which is more like apathy.

Seven

COMMUNICATION BARRIERS

My act is the price I pay for my safety and my strokes. It is the armor that protects me from getting hurt, but it is also a barrier within myself that stunts my growth. Likewise it is a wall between us that will prevent you from getting to know the real me.

John Powell, S.J.
Will The Real Me Please Stand Up? (1985)

Superficiality and Game-Playing *{When the face we know isn't the face we show....}*

It is fairly common to expect that upon initially meeting someone, we won't know *all* that a person is. In fact, we probably get the *best* possible picture. Somehow we are afraid that if we reveal all that we are in a first meeting, without some measure of defense or guard, we might destroy our chances of ever seeing the person again.

This is the reason we so often engage in a type of "game playing" when we begin a romance. It can have to do with portraying ourselves as very popular or in demand with others, perhaps more than we really are. This might be done in an effort to prove or establish our worth as a person, to have us appear valuable, so that our partner feels fortunate and makes more of an effort to connect and remain with us.

While that may seem to work in the short term, it will inevitably backfire. No one is able to hold out their "real" selves long enough to fool someone forever. Whether it is subconscious or a consciously motivated strategy, it is bound to set you up to fail. Besides, why wouldn't you want someone to love *you*? The *REAL* you?

Here again, both sexes complain. The female side of the argument is that men oversell who they are, portraying themselves as something they are not. Men call women "plastic" as they dress to attract with their attention-getting make-up and accoutrements. We have all lived through these accusations, or at least have heard the stories.

But in listening to such comments, how can we not consider the *cause*, once again, for people feeling the need to engage in such roguish dating behaviors? Men must feel that they need to misrepresent their positions in life because that will determine whether or not the woman is interested, whether she will continue talking to him or not. I guess the object of the game is to lure her into falling in love with him 'under the guise,' and then once she's hooked on his irresistible charm and personality, it won't matter that he isn't really an M.D., but in reality a janitor for the local high school.

Similarly, a woman who gets a bad rap for all her makeup, etc, is attempting with all she has to play dress-up to attract her man. Once she has him, the inevitable moment will arrive in which he sees her without her painted beauty, wearing sweats, at home, perhaps demonstrating her not-so-plastic behaviors.

In the book entitled, *Smart Women, Foolish Choices*, Dr. Cowan and Dr. Kinder write:

Single people complain...about the predictable quality of the first encounter. 'Nothing feels fresh anymore.' They explain that the opening lines, the topics raised, even the jokes at singles bars and other singles *meeting places are stale and boring. The real problem, of course, is that people are afraid to let go and be themselves. In another setting, where they felt more comfortable and open, these same people might prove to be much more interesting.(*p144).

Isn't it a complete wonder that the very thing men and women get crazy complaining about in the opposite sex, is the exact thing that they initially *sought after* in a mate? Something is wrong here. It may have to do with truth in advertising.

For example, I have known women who have married men with terrific jobs, some physicians, others, business executives. Whether or not they set out to hook husbands with financial security is unknown. (Only a few have actually admitted that they have.) In any case, there they are in all their worldly comfort, angry that they are alone much of the time, lonely, often competing for their husband's attention. They long for the "sensitive" type, the one they had *not* been attracted to because wealth, power, and status are not what he is about. For these men, their *personal* lives took precedence. And now, the woman with the unlimited toys envies the one who has prince charming as a best friend and soul mate.

I have also known men who have married a woman who meets their "standard" of physical appeal, even though they may have accused these women of phony behavior. But now they refer to her as 'high maintenance,' and don't like all the time it takes for her to get ready to go out.

So, what is it that makes us *want* to engage in such deceitful, distracting game playing to attract and interest someone? Women say they are weary of the tired pick up lines. Once men get what they want, the compliments aren't so forthcoming. Men ask why women get all made up and pretend they don't eat on a date. The truth comes out once they 'get their claws into' you; they let themselves go, wear sweats, and you see how much they *really* eat! No one truly wants to deceive anyone, because we all want to be liked for precisely who we are. But somehow, we feel we have to. Competing in the world of dating means putting our best foot forward, even if it means only while we are engaged in the chase.

So often it seems that we are virtually compelled to play in the mating/dating game. We are motivated to do this because of what we *expect* to happen. It is a defense. Defenses are always based on some *fear*, which we already know is False Evidence only *Appearing* Real. For example, men fear rejection and so use pick up lines as a cover because it's easier to laugh off when rejected. Women think they can't eat in the company of their prospective mate because somewhere, at some time, they got a message that it's unfeminine to eat. Could that be right? Besides, they have to maintain the image *expected* of them: women are supposed to eat daintily, to watch their weight. Thin is in; any body fat at all threatens our security. God forbid we "let ourselves go!"

Being rejected by someone is nothing to fear, it doesn't have any power over validating us as a good, worthy person. And exhibiting a healthy appetite during a date doesn't make us undesirable as a female partner. When we write this and read it, it all sounds so obvious. Nevertheless, what happens is that we are usually dealing at a strong emotional level. That's why it's false evidence *appearing* real…it appears that way in our feelings' state, not the conscious, thinking, rational one.

The problem is that these expectations of ours could have no basis in truth. We may have already accused our date of a stereotypical notion, when they have absolutely no intention of rejecting us, or judging our profession or the way we eat. That's why if we aren't looking for something outside ourselves to validate our worth, it's unlikely that we will have these erroneous expectations based in fear.

Whether or not we begin with little white lies designed to attract someone to us, it is always a mistake to put that person in charge of meeting our needs. We set ourselves up for failure because when we expect, especially unrealistically, we run the risk of disappointment. Disappointment always sets us up to feel like victims, powerless over what has happened *to us*. We may not have control over what happens, but we should know that we always have control over how we respond to what happens.

The other possibility is predicated on subconscious attraction. Perhaps we are sending signals of attraction to the individual whom we would like to "fix," or the one with whom we can address an unresolved issue. Remember, this is a challenging attraction, one that may cause two people great pain and heartache. It is far better to have done our inside work so that when we are ready, we attract a healthy relationship rather than one which will undeniably mean hard work and frustration with little hope for the future. The clarity gained from work with the self prior to a new relationship would save us a good deal of time, energy, and expense.

When we are role playing, or pretending we are someone we are not, we don't help ourselves in the relationship game. We don't succeed in "fooling" anyone long term and misrepresenting ourselves always creates additional anxiety. Isn't there already enough angst attached to meeting someone new?

This kind of behavior may translate to some lack of self-esteem. We usually try to be someone else when we do not like who we really are. So, begin there. Fix that liking yourself stuff. You'll never want to be anyone else ever again. You will come to realize that you are perfect, just the way you are, just the way you were made. Attracting the "right" person will not necessarily need to be a deliberate, planned effort. *It will just happen.*

Sex Language Barriers

When women go to bed with a man on a first date or soon thereafter, they may be interpreting the man's advances {through their own perceptual screen} as love or at least an act of emotional bonding. Perhaps it is because they think they are *supposed* to interpret it that way. Neither of these reasons is very good or caring to ourselves as women of dignity and self-respect. It is non-supportive and tends to diminish our own importance to the man and to ourselves.

When men get to the bed scene quickly, it normally has to do with physical attraction; we already know that men are highly visual. Other reasons could range from pure ego lust to testing the waters. If you do, he may even lose interest, and if you don't, he feels challenged ... perhaps only for the time being.

We can see how sex not only "gets in the way," but until it's *out* of the way, we sometimes feel the relationship can not commence. In truth, it is the exact opposite. Until we can be friends, get to know and care about one another without the sex, we will not be able to have meaningful lovemaking. Assuming that none of us really wants "just sex" in the end, but rather to "make love" with someone we care about and *love*, it is crucial that we are clear on the best way to achieve this end. Always have the relationship *before* you have the sex.

The gender sex drama is both intriguing and very telling. It is personified dominance and submission. In order for a man to feel sexual, it is necessary for him to be and feel the aggressor, in most cases. In order for the woman to feel "womanly," she feels she must somehow be in service to her man. That is exemplified in the typical submission on her part in the sex act.

In an old book by Julius Fast entitled, *The Incompatibility of Men and Women*, he makes a case for this kind of symbolism. He uses a man's erection and penetration as the sign of aggression; the idea of woman's being penetrated as the sign of submission.

He even goes on to suggest that female submissiveness is really a fear that actually makes women not only able to, but also willing to have sex. On the other hand, if a man feels fear, he is virtually incapable of completing the sex act. That's probably what performance anxiety is all about. If a man feels as if he is being ordered to perform and becomes fearful that he will not or cannot, it becomes a self-fulfilling prophecy. If a woman feels anger, which is a reaction typically associated with male aggression, it precludes her from feelings of sexual desire. The way it is, says Julius Fast, is our biological and cultural inheritance.

The author discusses what is beneath all this, that which causes the drama in the first place. He strongly suggests why men truly have a vested interest in keeping things just as they have always been with the gender status. At issue is men's underlying fear that women want to take over, considered a continual challenge to their manhood. Fast refers to women as the "classic castrator," inferring that it is in man's best interest to keep control, lest women get their wish.

The language of sex, meaning what is said through the physical attraction state all the way to the act itself, presents another potential barrier in the effort for men and women to communicate. It is probably not a good idea to offer any particular recommendation, as with so many things it is individual. Still, we must know that the most fulfilling kind of sexual enjoyment has to come when two people have done a good job of caring for each other and it culminates in physical expression.

Do people cheat because of some Biological or other Need for Sex??

We have already mentioned that there is no such thing. We have discussed the mythological belief that anyone should *need* sex. No one has ever expired due to a dissatisfactory, inadequate, or non-existent sex life.

Anyone, male or female, who cheats on a mate usually is dealing with one of four problems:

1. Pure insecurity; a "spare" is needed in the event one is abandoned. Also, could be a need to "prove" something.
2. He/She is working out a psychological drama whereby they "auto-

matically" have multiple relationships, duplicating some past history (what they saw, knew, or came to understand is acceptable).

3. A subconscious attempt to avoid intimacy. True commitment is threatening because of its intimacy demands on us. If that kind of closeness is scary, it is likely because we are not familiar with real relationships. Usually, someone like this successfully avoids intimacy by having both people in his or her life.

4. The other issue, of course, is a function of the particular committed relationship in which one finds himself or herself. If one's needs are not being met inside this relationship, then it is possible to stray, erroneously believing that a new partner is the answer.

Intentions may be to have this new situation work out, therefore paving the way to leave the old, or simply to avoid facing the problems within the committed relationship. Either way, it is not the recommended procedure to ending a union with another. We are far better to understand that finding a new love will never fix what was wrong with us inside a relationship (and we *do* play a role in whatever does not work out). Facing, instead, what *is* wrong, taking action to fix it, first within ourselves, then possibly within the union, is much more productive and sure to yield longer term satisfaction and inner peace.

Some people also have some difficulty with the thought of being with one person for the rest of their lives. They may feel that it is impractical, presents a real potential for boredom. I have heard some people come to the conclusion that it may even be "unnatural." The alternative, however, may prove to be harry; we grow wearier of this as we get older.

People who intentionally select unavailable partners get to hide behind a facade and not face their fear. This may be a fear of intimacy. We see this when previously unavailable people suddenly become available, only to scare off their regular dating partner. They will either sabotage the relationship or panic, usually meaning they exit.

We want to understand what is called the platinum rule: *Do unto others as they would have you do unto them.* We must all be willing and prepared to meet people at their personal level of need instead of ours. Being sensitive to who they are while at the same time being able to communicate so that they can hear us is a skill that we can learn when we care enough to make it work.

Speaking of communication, we all know how good it feels to be complimented, especially when there is little question that it is sincere and there is no hidden agenda. In dating, we innately understand how compliments are part of the game. A man may understand it from the hunting/conquer perspective, but a woman also has ideas on what a man needs to hear, and when it is real, she should readily compliment him. Of course, we need to take care about not sounding too patronizing, but it's unlikely to happen if it is honest. This may be a good example…of all the lines that I've heard and heard about, here is a personal favorite:

A Favorite Compliment

Many of us have been told that we are pretty, handsome, sexy, etc., but the best compliment I ever received was after I helped someone with a problem, he turned to me and said "How did you get so smart?" We probably couldn't underestimate the impact of such a thought...and the value of it is certainly long lasting. I loved it and never forgot it. When I think about all the "wasted" lines ever used, I smile to myself, knowing that I can not be the only woman in the world who would rather be complimented on something that really matters.

The reason I liked it so much was because I felt it was so genuine and sincere. Since the hunter instinct says that there may have been a goal attached to the compliment, he may have had a purpose for saying what he said. It wasn't at all evident, however. It was refreshing and sweet, and if we had both been single at the time, I guess I would've thought of it as rather alluring. Men should know that women, even very attractive women, don't always want men to tell them how pretty they are. They usually already know that, anyway. What they'd prefer to know is what the man specifically likes about them, not on the surface, but *them*, as individuals, their spirit and essence.

It's the same with men. Everyone wants to be appreciated for who they are, not always for what they look like or what they have. There is just a greater receptivity in receiving a compliment that is real, truthful, and doesn't have anything to do with our face or body parts.

As a matter of fact, whenever we wish to give a compliment, we need to know that it sounds a good deal more sincere if we are specific about what it is we like. If we just say, "You look nice," it can seem gratuitous. Saying instead that I really love the way you look when your hair is up, sounds definite enough to be honest and real.

THE "UNAPPROACHABLE BEAUTY":

To men: When her body language turns you off and turns you away...

From women: Here's the question: "I don't get approached very often when I'm out. What's wrong?"

Consider this, ladies. If you walked into a bar and saw two men, equally attractive, both well dressed, appearing to be alone. Man A is smiling, nothing presumptuous, but seemingly open and friendly; the other, Man B, sits with his arms crossed on his chest, looking fairly serious, making no eye contact. Which man would you be more likely to approach?

If you responded Man A, you are like the rest of us who are encouraged or discouraged by body language cues. What we sometimes fail to realize is that we are constantly giving off signals, possibly telling people who we are and what we are thinking all the time. With experts warning us of the 55% impact of non-verbal communication, there is no doubt that in our silence we speak volumes. More important than *what* we say is often *how* we say it and the subconscious 'language' in which our bodies are engaged at the time.

This is not unknown to us. As we said before, we are interpreting non-verbal messages every day, several times a day. Think of the times when we meet someone, perhaps for the first time, and as we begin to walk away from this individual, a feeling overcomes us ... we may not even know *why*... but we do know *what*: We know whether or not we feel good about this person. We may refer to it as a "gut feeling." It is intuition, a treasure that many of us may not rely on *enough*.

So, what do we do? First, it wouldn't be a bad idea to become somewhat aware of the language of the body. This is both for more conscious interpretation of other people and for self-awareness purposes. Know that any barrier placed between you and another individual projects a possible defensive posture. Whether this is a piece of furniture or a part of your body (as with the crossed arms), the message is a warning that friendship, much less intimacy, is *not* being invited.

That is pretty straight-forward. We need to look also to the eyes and total body positioning as they can help provide additional cues to either support/reinforce or negate your immediate (gut) evaluation. In other words, do not make the mistake of interpreting any gesture in isolation. The total picture is what is important. If an individual happens to cross arms and avoid eye contact, his feet pointing in a direction away from you, these would be considered congruous gestures. Even if he were verbalizing otherwise, I would be inclined to believe that there is little genuine interest here.

We do not need to become experts. Certain simple bits of information can be very handy to have when we are unsure, even if it serves only to reinforce what our reliable 'gut' tells us.

Reading boredom signals and lack of confidence gestures are somewhat second nature to us, perhaps because we encounter them rather regularly. A child doodling and a 'fish' handshake have long been offering us clues for reading a person non-verbally. Still, we do need to be mindful of what the experts call *gesture clusters* in establishing congruity.

It is said that a smile is the best way to show acceptance of another person. We must all learn to smile more. It not only makes the receiver feel good, it'll get us feeling positive as well. A firm handshake isn't only "good business-practice," it lends an air of self-confidence. Eye contact allows us to feel comfortable with one another; it expresses sincerity as well as interest and trust. An open body posture invites others toward us, while closed body positions or crossed arms, legs, and hands sends others away.

Men may not always recognize this, but when a particularly attractive woman "looks" disinterested, it is often a defense. Perhaps she has been approached before and she gave her heart to the wrong man. It is possible that she is self-conscious (yes, I know that she is attractive, but not all attractive people are self-confident), and needs a less abrasive approach. She may have had some kind of negative experience in the past that caused her to develop this posture in order to protect herself. She could have learned, as Thomas Moore explains in SoulMates, "that the courage required to open (her) soul to receive another is infinitely more demanding than the effort (she puts) into avoidance...(p30)." Throw away your used-up lines and strike up a genuine conversation that does not involve sex in the first twenty sentences. Be real with her, and if she rejects you anyway, it's okay, because it probably would not have worked. Look at it as having saved two people an awful lot of time and trouble.

For both sexes, here is the caveat:

If you really wish to convey an appearance of confidence, friendliness and approachability, you will need to *convince yourself first*. We have already discussed how our body signals depend on our self-image, the picture we hold in our minds about who we are. We cannot dictate our body language at the conscious level. Our thoughts and feelings are passed directly from the subconscious to the body. That's why our body language is so honest; it does not check in with the conscious mind to evaluate the decision or course of action.

This should make it easier to understand why we cannot attract the "wrong person" when we are right with ourselves, since we attract only those who meet with our dominant thoughts about who we are. It is automatic; the signal goes directly from internal feelings to outward behavior. We need to tell ourselves that we are a friendly, willing, and open prospect -- believe it, and our body will follow, portraying that message in physical position to all those around us.

Experts in the field claim that if what we believe and what we are saying are inconsistent, our body language will blow our cover and give us up. It will reveal our truest feelings and attitudes, sending the most believable message of the two. The body does not lie. Because non-verbal language is entirely less-than-conscious, it does not pass through the thinking and evaluation stage prior to behaving, rendering the raw truth behind any facade.

Here are 8 quick points worth remembering about Non-verbal Communication:

1. Our bodies do not lie!
2. Our thoughts will get expressed.
3. We convey feelings through our attitudes displayed in our behavior.
4. The attitude causes the gesture to occur; prolonging the gesture forces the attitude to remain.

5. When we say things we do not mean, we non-verbally communicate what we really feel about it.
6. When verbal and non-verbal are incongruent, the non-verbal signals will carry about five times the impact.
7. Remember that our subconscious works to complete the picture we put in it (through our self-concept and self-esteem).
8. Change the picture first; the behavior will follow the picture!

Sometimes, communication barriers take the form of cliches and tired phrases that somehow get perpetuated over time. Most often, they reflect our habits, patronizing thoughts, and unfortunately, shallow beliefs about what we "should" do and be, as if there really are such standards or expectations. Again, we are so afraid to be real, to be who we are, that we hide behind these phrases to explain our "other" person to the world.

THE 6 Most Annoying Phrases Heard:

I see these as communication barriers because they are disingenuous and lacking in individual thought:

1. **"But *everyone* is getting married!"**

This attitude is the kiss of death because it sets the stage for what we ought to call "settling." We all know people who should never have been married. These folks marry, removing themselves from the opportunity to meet other eligible partners, and all because they were in a hurry, thought there was "no one left," or whatever the many not-nearly-good-enough reasons.

People have a tendency to jump on the bandwagon when they fail to listen to their own personal inner voice. This is because we cannot know what is in our hearts when we fail to listen. When we aren't listening, we can find ourselves confused. Our confusion may cause us to make mistakes. These are the kind of avoidable mistakes that happen when we just go through the motions, deny ourselves quiet time, think that everyone else must have the answers.

When we think of such a comment as "everyone's doing it," it sounds suspiciously lacking in self-trust. A lack of faith in oneself is usually accompanied by a faith in something *outside* oneself that can lead us down a path of falsehood. Listen instead to your internal guidance; it has been with you all the time just waiting for you to ask for help.

{not everyone HAS TO marry, either...}

Trust yourself, then you will know how to live.
Goethe, Proverbs in Prose, 1828

Believe it or not, there are some people who never have married, nor do they ever wish to marry. They aren't necessarily unhappy people. Single people have no reason to feel inadequate, guilty, or coerced into jumping on bandwagons. It is entirely possible that their plight in life takes them in a direction in which having a family could be an impediment.

Still, while we may not need to be married, or even have a romantic partner, we do need contact with other humans. Friends are the next best things to family—sometimes even better!

I spoke to many single people, ones who never married to those who have experienced divorce. Some had weekend relationships and others had long distance relationships, seeing each other only a few times each year. None of the individuals I interviewed were unhappy about their arrangements. By and large, they spoke quite positively about it, and assured me that they liked it just the way it was. Many did mention the demise of friends' marriages and the associated difficulty that came with the legal entanglement. While this may have seemed a logical justification, it did not appear to prevent them from remaining open-minded about the possibility of commitment. It simply was not their *objective.*

2. **It takes "too much effort" to have a relationship...**{I'm too tired to bother}

If this is what you believe, there is no doubt you will or have already proven yourself absolutely correct. There is truth to the statement that a relationship is not always easy. It is work, but a good relationship is well worth the effort.

I heard so many people express exhaustion at the thought of a new relationship. They expended all their energy on the one that just ended, and it is quite possible that the next relationship will require a similar amount of energy only to end the same way. Wrong!!! Not if you figure it out first. From what I could see, many of the people expressing such exasperation were the same ones who stayed much too long, tried much too hard, often with little to no effort on the part of their partner. They tried so hard to please that they gave up who they were and lost themselves in the process. That's the issue. That's what was so exhausting. Why do we place ourselves in a position where we refuse to give up, even when it is obvious that the relationship is lifeless or even abusive?

There's an old adage that says anything worth it is never easy. Sometimes it will seem as if being in a relationship is the most difficult of all life's challenges. But, the rewards are many and wonderful. That kind of connection with another provides a sense of security and warmth that is difficult to imagine one could obtain elsewhere.

We may also have arrived at a point where if we've been there and done that, we cannot possibly 'do it' again. Better to live alone and single. This is understandable, but there's another way to look at it. When we love, our gift to the one we love may be our example. It may seem too easy to think that you may influence someone with your actions alone, but that may be how they learn to see whatever they need to. You may be just 'what the Good Doctor ordered' to move this person along in an unconditionally loving relationship. After all, our placement in people's lives is purposeful. There are no "accidents." The only thing that is necessary to understand is that we should not "do it again" until we feel good about where we are first. This means we stop looking back to our past and love ourselves first before we ask anyone to share in our lives.

3. A Hard Time Saying "No"

In the process of seeking a life partner, we will meet many frogs (not meant as a physical qualifier), and the inability to say no can pose undesirable consequences. It's one thing to be nice, but we never have to be agreeable at the expense of our self-esteem. We can learn to say 'No' in a non-threatening, caring way, which makes our message lovingly clear and reaffirms our self-worth at the same time.

One of the reasons this would be an issue is that we do not believe we have the right to say no. We may hide behind the "I'm too nice" routine or "I can't hurt his feelings," or even a misunderstanding: "I said yes, but I didn't mean let's get serious, I meant yes, a date sounds good...." In addition to not being self-supportive, not being able to assert one's disinterest is misleading and unfair to the other person.

Say, for example, that an individual has trouble rejecting offers from the opposite sex. There is little chance we can be learn to be monogamous if we continually agree to date multiple people. It does generally take restraint and morality and even common sense to turn away from temptation. Unfortunately, it is rather necessary, if we are ever to achieve success at a long term committed relationship.

In terms of getting the message across to someone who wants to see us, nothing does the job quite as well as the word "NO" does it. If we need to, we take an assertiveness training class. We owe it to ourselves to not fear standing up for who we are. It never means we have to feel bad, or mad, or guilty ... it only means we get to be us without unfavorable consequences. Besides, in the end we are all more respected for the self-respect we exhibit.

Here's a final word on the topic of honesty in communications with another:

John Powell, author of several good self-help books wrote in *Why Am I Afraid to tell You Who I am?:*

Most of us feel that others will not tolerate such emotional honesty in communication. We would rather defend our dishonesty on the grounds that it might hurt others; and, having rationalized our phoniness into nobility, we settle for superficial relationships.

No one would actually admit to preferring a "superficial relationship." We simply find ourselves there one day, hopefully prior to marrying the person, and we decide that we need to feel emotionally connected to our partner. If a relationship is superficial, we want the person to be an acquaintance, not a spouse, not even a "friend."

When we fail to be honest with another and especially with ourselves, we dishonor who we truly are and end up in situations where we are less than happy with the outcome. We do not have anyone else to blame, as we have made choices. Both our happiness and peace of mind are our gifts to ourselves.

4. **(But) She/he has such a "Nice Personality"...**

Most of us have heard people say, sometimes in the presence of one being spoken about, that the person's best asset is their personality. Both men and women recognize this patronizing assessment. The implication is that unfortunately while "good looks" may not be exactly an accurate description, the lovely personality is a close second asset.

This happens more to women than it does men, of course, because again, society's standards are much harsher on women when it comes to our physical package. Men, we recall, can easily possess compensatory assets such as money, power, and position. People feel they need to justify and defend their son's marriages with his wife's personality, much like they have justified their daughter's decision to marry the ogre of a superstar athlete or tycoon.

We are far better off not doing anyone any favors to compliment them in this backhanded manner. In other words, if you have nothing good to say, don't say anything. If beauty is truly in the eyes of the beholder, then why even qualify a prospect. Leave it be, up to the one to whom it may matter. Our looks-conscious society has made us neurotic. We may all eventually come to the inevitable realization that this "cover" is merely one of our tests. We *learn* from having bodies. Otherwise, we really wouldn't need them. We would be communicating mind to mind, spirit to spirit, and we'd all be equals.

5. "I just want to be friends"...

Can we love someone of the opposite sex, and NOT wish to marry him or her?

Falling in Like…or falling for love?

There is a difference. There will be times in our lives when we like someone but we do not love them, or we are not in love with them. And only because they are a member of the opposite sex may it be questioned. Is this a friendship? Can an opposite sex couple be "just friends?" When we love someone, there is little question that we like them also, even though we may not always like what they do. But when we like someone and they happen to be of the opposite sex, there looms an inevitable threat of romantic potential. Can we have a friendship despite all this tension? The "difference" begs acknowledgment.

So, how do we know when it is love, or friendship? Can we ever ensure requited feelings between two people? We need to know the difference, but how can we tell when we "fall"? And *what does* that mean, really? Where are we, *how* are we "falling"...? And when do we stop, you know, get up, pick up, whatever? It's no wonder that we refer to it as falling--the dictionary definition is to "go lower, be defeated or ruined, commit a sin."

When Harry met Sally in the movie, they began as friends. They really liked each other, but had no inkling that they could be romantically involved ... until they had had enough discussions and interacted enough to realize that they had very similar values. They were seeking the same attributes in a suitable partner. Their "falling in love" was less like a plunge and more like a gradual decent into ... comfort.

In time, Harry and Sally had come to know one another enough not to be clouded over by the deceptive condition of the typical and often overrated infatuation that takes place on a first, second, or even third date. I mean, how much can we know about a person in that short a time? When we take the time to nurture the relationship without that cloud of deception, we are able to move into whatever is to be the next stage of development.

Some relationship experts think that we fall in love with a fantasy of a person. This means that sooner or later, when that individual exposes his humanness, we will be let down, disappointed. We must be careful what we are so eager to call love.

Of course, we can love without being in love romantically. There is generally so much pain associated with this because ideally we all want to love the person we like so much, just as we want to *like* the person we are 'in love' with. In reality, we love a great number of individuals; we can be in love with only one person at a time. We want to have it all with our life partner: we want to like them, be in love with them, *and love* them. The love is truly the mainstay of the relationship; being *in love* is a phase that will come and go, swept up in emotions of the many moments we will experience together.

We will not, nor could we ever have a romantic relationship with everyone of the opposite sex we befriend. It would be neither practical nor meaningful. But this male/female friendship dilemma is very real for some of us. There is an invisible wall that is erected between many couples who wish to remain friends, but know that somehow, '*it' could happen.*

I think we all understand how confusing this may be. It would seem that a prerequisite to a good relationship is a solid friendship between the couple. But what we call friendship is really love. Without that kind of foundation, it is conceivable that a marriage will not stand the test of time. We must be able to talk honestly to one another, laugh together, and provide the other with support and unconditional love and acceptance. Without that, we have fertile ground for disappointment and frustration in any relationship.

We all know there are times when we like a person, even a great deal, but we are not in love with them. It can be unfortunate when feelings are not mutual, when only one of the two of you wishes for the relationship to grow into a romance. But it does not, in fact, should not mean that we have to lose the friendship. It may take some time, but eventually, this kind of platonic relationship can return to a lifelong friendship. Do not give up. That kind of love eventually works its way out.

Finally, it is possible that we can like and love a person and not like what he/she does. Whether this is the romantic kind of relationship, or the friendship, we will recognize this kind of conflict. Not approving of someone's actions is not the same as not loving them; the two are mutually exclusive. The gamut of emotions can run through the disapproval, but our love remains constant. This is how we can hate the behavior and not the person. And this is the distinction that is critical when we communicatc our disapproval.

There is no way to ensure our love will be requited. We may end up loving someone who thinks of us as only a friend, or vice versa. That is, we could wish to be mere friends with someone who feels a romantic attachment with us. Unless the feelings are mutual, there is no sense in spending a great deal of time trying to force the issue. It was not meant to be; if we can remain friends, we should do so. It is likely that it will prove to be a valuable friendship. If we simply cannot manage a friendship immediately, we might separate for the time we need. The time will come when we are able to resume what we once had. It will come, and we will be pleased that we did not close the door permanently.

6. I have to find myself...I don't know who I am yet, I need my space

When we hear these trite expressions, we sometimes roll our eyes in disbelief. We think it is an easy way out, a cop out, a cover for something that cannot be said for fear of hurt feelings. Why don't you just tell me, we think. We both know *why*-- I'm not good enough, I don't make enough money, You want someone far more attractive, I'm too heavy...

We almost feel as if it would be easier to take if the person would only just say it. But would the "truth" really make it any easier? Perhaps the irony in our desire to hear the truth is because those are the things that make sense to us. We just "knew it"; we weren't good enough. We get to *prove ourselves right.*

Hearing the conciliatory comment that it's not us, our partner just needs to find himself or herself, *can* be insulting. Just when we think we have found the person of our dreams, they need to discover the meaning of life! And if our self-esteem is vulnerable, it can cause depression or even serve as a devastating blow. But it is also possible that this person is doing you the greatest favor ever.

First of all, they may truly be "lost." If *they* "can't find" themselves, how will *you* ever expect to find them, get to know them. Sure, some just use this handy line just to get us off their backs or to soften the blow of a direct rejection, but some people are truly feeling this way. Let them go.

And finally, something very special may be waiting for you just around the bend; how will you come to know this greatness if you are busy doing something less than what was intended for your life? No reflection on the particular individual, only in what you were personally meant for. Stop trying to control events; most things are simply unfolding in a very intentional sort of way.

Space is healthy. We all need "our space," and we need to respect one another's space. Even in marital union, where "two become one," we continue to be in our own skin -- responsible for our selves and for our individual responses to what occurs. Asking for space can in fact be a valuable contribution to a relationship as someone respects his or her own need to think.

It might be good to recall something written by the celebrated German author, Johann Wolfgang von Goethe:

When you love something, set it free. If it comes back, it's yours. If it doesn't, it never was.

Between a Doormat And the Burning Bra

searching for that female middle ground...

There is a simple rule of thumb we can all stand to live by: Whenever there exists an *extreme*, whenever a balance is upset due to a one way or an opposite...it is *never* positive. Doormats and burned bras are just that -- extremist positions. And they have the tendency to miscommunicate something about who we are inside.

Women have accomplished a great deal. Why is it so prevalent then, to find a large number caught between two extremes? Why can't women be women without having to burn their bras in protest and unfeminine activity, or at the other end, lay down and submit 100% to a man?

I know many women who are far from denying their femininity, yet they function very well in the world of men. They do not feel a need to be loud or make issues of things, debating, asserting, etc. They are not defensive, simply conduct their lives with grace and defenselessness.

The female double standard is almost as obnoxious as the male double standard in this country. Think of it. We all know countless examples of persistent male-domination in the world, but are we so quick to judge our feminine selves with our role in that persistence? How many women could honestly admit to wanting to be taken care of?

The reality is that women realize should they decide to have a family, the onus *will* be on them to raise the children. If done properly, this will take a great deal of time and energy. Even in the best of circumstances we are not sure that we *can* have it all and do it all. Probably for this reason alone, our preference is to find a man who can *afford* for us not to work. Instead of being up front with this, however, women "secretly" pursue the financially stable kind of man, while on the surface they continue to pretend that it is not important. They may be trying to save face with feminist sisters who would take exception to such traditional attitudes.

Before anyone else is going to be able to accept women as equal partners, at work *or* in the bedroom, women must first be convinced that they are equal and worthy of respect. Projecting self-love and self-respect is unmistakable. And, it's contagious. People will treat you consistent with how you feel about and thus treat yourself.

Extreme behavior is a signal. It is not about something outside ourselves to which we respond. It is about something inside, to which we *react* on the outside. Pointing a blaming finger is nothing but a smokescreen. Whether we are ardent feminists or completely submissive, it tells us that our self-esteem is not all it could be. The only way we ever feel threatened is when we are not sure of ourselves. If we truly believe we are 100% worthy and valuable, how can we be threatened?

A happy medium is automatic when we know who we are. We can't take on extremist attitudes with open-minded acceptance and self-love. We neither stir reactions in others nor give others permission to mistreat us, no matter what ... or how much we think we love. Knowing who we are and being true to that attracts people who are good for us and good to us.

If you still feel the need to burn your bra, just remember that there may come a time when you will need the support. And if you choose to be a doormat--and it *is* a choice, recognize that it will be a dirty, thankless job.

The case of Controlling Partners

We have already discussed how by nature, most men tend to enjoy control. These men need to feel as though they have control, as it is part of being male and experiencing power. But there are cases where both men and women have been carried away with the need to control, aggressively and passively.

In the beginning, it's almost cute that he's jealous. It's sweet that she wants you all to herself, and pouts when you do things without her. It's a compliment to most of us that someone loves us so much that they want to spend a good deal of time with us. He or she may even be very charming, sending flowers and buying us things to make us happy. All this is fine, within limits.

When that same man begins to severely restrict your activities and cannot understand why you need to spend time with your family and friends apart from him, or she begins to question what you do when, how, or why, better be careful. Someone who needs control generally has a problem, and loving you only exacerbates their problem. It is possible that this person is incapable of love, even as he or she vehemently proclaims it for you. Feelings of insecurity may preclude true feeling of love for another.

No one is undeserving of love, of course. It's just that this is an individual who needs help before they are ready for a relationship. These people tend to be psychologically clever, so someone dating them would need to stay one step ahead. Know the warning signs of someone who needs this kind of power in a relationship-- signs of abuse and control. Here are some to consider:

- Someone who either aggresively or passively manages to get their own way in the end. Being right is too important to them.
- Someone who seems to believe that their ideas and decisions are always better than another person's.
- Someone who is demanding, needing to get what he or she wants, possibly downplaying your needs. This includes cutting you off from people who love you.
- Someone who is vengeful—can not seem to let go when he or she feels wronged.

Remember that although these people may seem confident and assertive, underneath the surface they are afraid that they are not lovable. That's why they're trying to control the situation, because they believe if left up to chance, they won't get love. If you do love someone like this, try to understand and encourage them to love's awareness and possibly therapeutic help.

Being drawn to someone who is controlling may be a function of your personal battle with feelings of abandonment and low self-worth. If you are dependent on this person for security or just to feel important, then you may be a candidate for therapy of your own. This is that subconscious attraction we have been discussing, and it will not change unless you do something about it and help yourself first. Remember that no one can do anything to us without our consent. That isn't philosophy, it is fact.

Listening with The Heart

Over the years, comedians have made a great deal of money at the expense of the opposite sex, and why not? It *is* funny. We can laugh uproariously about how we fail to understand why men's and women's needs are so very "different." We may even take to reading those books that successfully point out how male and female thinking is so dissimilar that we may as well be from different planets.

What is at the heart of the issue is really a lost art-- an under-taught and absolutely crucial skill, that of *LISTENING*. It isn't so much that men and women are so different from each other as much as it is that we need to listen more *and* better to one another. When we listen actively to what another is saying it not only increases our comprehension, but it also demonstrates to the speaker that we *care* and that they are *worth* our time and trouble. That *alone* will improve our relationships!

A vast number of relationship complaints stem from a deficient ability to hear our partner out and demonstrate a degree of concern and perhaps empathy. We all need to feel as though we are being listened to, that what we feel matters. This is where all the talk of "mirroring" comes in during therapy sessions. Mirroring demonstrates empathy as we restate our understanding of what has been expressed/communicated and shared by our mate. When all else fails, though, listening alone -- not saying a word -- is always better than throwing up our hands, chalking up our inability to understand to basic gender differences.

If each of us did nothing more than become observant and more sensitive to one another's needs, we may be able to avoid many mistakes. Same sex friendships may even teach us a good deal of what we need to know. Women discuss, they meet for coffee or lunch and they talk. Men "touch base"; when they talk, it's about sports or a game, their game, etc.. Women need the intimacy factor to feel close, the emotional intimacy. Men need the physical closeness and an ear when they have a focus for a conversation, but do not usually have the emotional attachment that women do. Both need to be supported, but differently, having different expectations and ways of evaluating the success of an interaction. And neither really cares for unsolicited advice. Try to listen without the need to advise.

There is no question about men and women being different. Not only has nature ensured that fact, but gender differences also allow us to have unique experiences and to experience things differently. The truth is that even as this happens, we are *still* able to get in touch with how the other perceives. This is not only so that we increase our understanding and empathy for the opposite sex, but also so that we do not take our differences so personally and let them get in our way. We can still live and coexist peaceably.

Whether you are on a first date or in a relationship for awhile, it is always important to be a good listener. Here are a few points to consider in order to become an effective listener:

1. Concentrate on what your partner is saying; make a conscious effort to really listen.
2. Resist distractions, placing all irrelevant issues out of your mind. Avoid thinking about what you want to say while the other speaks.
3. Use eye contact. It tells the speaker that you are interested and sincere.
4. Arrange what you hear into key thoughts and feelings being conveyed by the speaker. This helps you avoid taking things out of context. You are after the *meaning* of what is being said.
5. Try to put yourself in the speaker's place. This establishes empathy and helps increase understanding of the speaker's intention and point of view. It also helps mitigate judgment.
6. Use a mirroring technique to check back with the speaker. In mirroring, we listen to what the speaker says and then paraphrase it back accurately. This assists in confirming and clarifying the meaning of your partner's words.

Do Not

1. Become distracted by doing anything while you are trying to listen. The goal is to give undivided attention to your partner.
2. Judge what is being said. If you allow it, your feelings about what is being said will negatively affect your listening.

3. Pull certain words or facts out of context. Remember that you are listening to what is being communicated in its entirety.
4. Interrupt the speaker before he or she is finished.
5. Express immediate agreement or disagreement. Just concentrate and wait.
6. Assume you understand right away.
7. Do most of the talking; you can't talk and listen at the same time. We have two ears and only one mouth for a perfectly good reason; we need to listen twice as much as we talk. We learn much more that way.

Whenever people feel really listened to, they end up thinking that the listener is the greatest...and when asked how the date went with this individual, reports are consistent... they had a terrific time!

♥ ♥ ♥

DateNotes

- "Playing the field" and "playing games" might be okay for people who aren't interested in making a serious impression for the purposes of a serious relationship. We all deserve the right to know the truth and usually with a topic like dating, we need to be aware of the other person's intent. As long as we have similar objectives, then no one has to get hurt.

- If sex is how men show their love and love is how women can do sex, then maybe we should all be more sensitive to what the other needs. If you don't know what to do, how or when to do it, then why not ask instead of trying to read minds and take the chance of getting it right.

- People usually do not cheat if they are happy and satisfied. Since it takes two to make a relationship, own up to your end of the deal by taking an active role in making it work. If you are paying attention, chances are that you would catch a problem before it becomes fatal.

- Don't assume that people who look good are confident and don't assume that they have no interest in you because they look a little too serious. Instead of waiting for them to smile or "look interested," why not smile yourself. If you do that and there is still little interest shown, then you might want to stop there. You might also want to consider saying something to make them laugh or doing something clever. There is no harm done and you have nothing to lose other than what you decide you've lost.

- ♥ Look for congruency in gestures in order to interpret what is being communicated, but know that non-verbal communication is also unlikely to be controlled. Our body gives us away as it "says" what it feels.

- ♥ Make it a point to be genuine whenever you communicate. Whether it is to give a compliment or to convey something, especially when important to another person, it is always best to be honest. Most people do appreciate this, even if the truth hurts for the immediate moment. What they remember is not that you didn't want them, but that you were sincere and had a reason for taking a particular stand.

- ♥ Take note of the recent example in New York City when the woman with the one hundred twenty-five thousand dollar wedding was stiffed on her wedding day. It was a cowardly act, no doubt, for the groom to bail out the way he did. Wouldn't it have been so much better if he had had the gumption to face her with the fact that he did not want to go through with it prior to the actual day? He had to have known at least one day previous. The end certainly would be the same (who would ever want a one-sided marriage, anyway?), but the means would have made him not appear so lacking in integrity.

- Women need to find their feminine middle ground. Extremes have never helped in maintaining good balance. Men and women are infinitely better off accepting each other for their differences and using them to their benefit.

- Know the signs of controlling partners. Whether it is aggressive emotional or physical abuse, or something more insidious like passive aggressive behavior, listen to friends who question it, and become educated on the subject to help yourself out of it. You are being attracted to this person because of something lacking in yourself.

- Listen in order to:
- Discover what the person wants (it's that sales technique again).
- Raise empathy;, as you hear what is being communicated, you are able to repeat and relay what was said, increasing your ability to understand and empathize.
- Nurture and satisfy the needs of your partner.

Eight

FINDINGS:
WHAT SINGLES TELL US

The results of our interviews, surveys and focus groups were not surprising. Most of what we found had reinforced what we had already learned from previous research and ongoing reports about dating, being single, and relationships. Still, it is interesting to report some of the data in light of what we attempt to accomplish here, specifically as it relates to using voice personals as a vehicle to meet and date people.

The first thing we want to note is that men and women do not appear to be all that different in what they want, what they fear, and how they evaluate prospects.

Composition of the Study:

Individuals who participated in the focus groups were solicited through a local newspaper, not on the same page that the voice personals ads appeared. They were invited if they were single, between ages 18 and 85, and were interested in participating in a session that would ask them to complete a questionnaire and discuss topics related to being single and dating. They were told that they would receive two tickets to the General Cinema and be entered in a $100.00 cash drawing at the end of the session. The results of their questionnaires and content of their feedback during that evening would be correlated with numerous in-depth and informal interviews that I had conducted over the course of a two year period. Even though the questionnaire provided specific multiple choice responses, participants were assured that they were not limited to only those answers. I would look to substantiate conclusions and findings of those interviews along with other semi-structured interview sessions that I had with people during the same time period. The percentages following reflect the cumulative result. Although I consistently attempted to interview a similar amount of men and women, in every case there were more women. The focus groups were comprised of about 60 percent females and 40 percent male. A similar breakdown occurred in each collection of interviews.

How Much Do Looks Matter?

In general, both genders held the values and philosophies of a prospective partner as the two highest priorities with looks consistently third, although men were slightly more slanted toward the importance of looks (24% to only 2% women).

In speaking to many individuals before, during, or after they responded to our questionnaire and participated in the focus groups, I discovered a perhaps loose definition of the word, "looks." Men seemed clear about the fact that they saw looks to be very important. One gentleman even wrote that he even felt "guilty about it," because he really thought that it was "the heart and personality that counts." Still, he admitted, "the first thing that happens when you meet someone is you see them. I don't know if being affected by looks is a natural thing for men, or if I just have a problem that I don't like in myself." Although it's true that he was representative, it is also evident that beauty is indeed in the eye of the beholder. Stereotypical models of beauty were the exception, not at all the rule. And interestingly, as women were reluctant to admit that looks was a high priority, they too admitted that it is an unavoidable attraction. Once again we come to see differences blur in what we like and are attracted to.

When we inquired about why men "liked good-looking women," 63% of men felt that it had to do with an envy of other men who see him with her, or that it was an "ego-extension," while fewer women, 47% thought that. Women gave more responsibility (53%) to men's superficiality and the notion that males were "visual creatures."

Looks resurfaced in response to the first thing that attracts us about someone. A majority of women (55%) responded that it was more the personality. And this was consistent with all other sources. Only 21% of men said it was personality first, with looks again, 43%, being selected as the majority response. This is also consistent.

Going Without a Partner

Although both groups mentioned the fear of being alone or lonely (54% of total), both groups tended to accept that it wasn't the worst that could happen. Subsequent discussions revealed that they acknowledge a general absence of stigma about being single, and a comfort level with their status.

Many of the interviewees mentioned that they know people who are married and are lonelier inside their marriages than they ever were without one, and found outlets for keeping busy either with friends or learning to do things alone. I found that people who tended to be more extroverted were more bothered by not having someone. That made sense, because as we now know, people like this tend to derive energy from the outside world, from being involved, getting out there and experiencing life.

To Pay or Not To Pay?

There was general agreement on the expectation of a woman offering to pay, splitting payment, or taking turns paying while out on a first date. (About 55% of women said this, while 75% of men felt this way.) And after two people had been dating for a few months, 87% of all respondents thought it was acceptable for a woman to offer, split, or take turns paying. This may somehow be reflective of the fact that today both parties are employed and therefore equally capable of picking up the tab. Still, while about 34% of females felt that a women need never pay on a first date, only 17% of men felt the same. Incidentally, men did not necessarily say that women *should* pay, only that they ought to make the offering gesture.

When asked to rank order priorities in a mate's characteristics, none of the men checked occupation in the list of important considerations, while 4% of the women did. Men generally did not care what a woman did, but if she was a "professional," it seemed they expected that she would work, or at least that she would want to work. Most women felt that a man both had to work and should do something that could support a family, although I was often assured that a 50/50 scenario was more than a fair arrangement, provided the household duties were split similarly.

The Assertive Role of the Female

Both genders perceived a woman calling a man as a positive move. Ninety percent of men and 79% of women saw her either as a confident individual or one unaffected by constraints of society, if there is such a thing about that today. None of the men were scared off by such a move from a woman although a few women (less than 1%) did believe that this would be frightening to a man. Still, this does blow the conventional "rules" of the courting game, that's for sure.

There was another confirmation of this. When asked what they would do if they found themselves very attracted to someone on a first date, both men and women said that they would initiate the next call. That could be considered somewhat modern as well, because convention would ask that the woman wait to be called or forget about the man.

Fear of Rejection

Men did seem to express a definitive fear of rejection, which wasn't surprising. For example, only 17% of men would take the risk and tell a woman that he was interested after a first date, while 32% of women would feel free to express themselves in this way. However, the majority of men, 67%, did indicate that they would initiate the call to get back together with someone, while only 42% of the women would.

In the past, women had no reason to fear being rejected because they merely waited to be asked, rather than put themselves out there doing the asking. Nevertheless, today I would imagine that there will be greater numbers of women sharing the same concerns as men, since they are also doing the asking. It will be interesting to see if women demonstrate greater resiliency towards the prospect of being rejected.

When asked about whether they would wait for the other person to call them after a successful first date, 35% of men thought they would wait as opposed to 63% of women. This seems to suggest that when given an option, women would rather be called, while men tended to take control and risk being turned down.

The clear distinction was in the willingness to verbally disclose interest. Men chose action over verbal disclosure, while women demonstrated a greater willingness to tell rather than act. This brings us back to traditional habits.

Non-verbal communication in Attraction

The critical importance of body language was also established both via questionnaires and in interviews. The reason most very attractive people do not get asked out is because they are emitting vibes that send people in another direction, away from approaching them. Over 50% of each group and 57% of the total respondents believed this. If we fail to smile, and perhaps make some eye contact, it is unlikely that we will get anyone to believe that they are invited to approach us. A smile is very important; most rated a smile as one of the first things they notice about someone, only slightly behind looks and personality for men, and just after personality for women. We might add that a smile is a good indicator of temperament, anyway.

On the"One Perfect Person" Theory

One confusing issue surfaced and was verified by the results of the interviews, feedback sessions, and questionnaires. People in general do tend to have some belief in this one perfect person notion. They were almost split between the idea that there is no one perfect, rather many potential prospects, with whom we could be happy, and the one and only theory. No one checked the "one ideal match waiting out there somewhere" theory on the questionnaire, however. What is curious is that, in light of the overwhelming challenge that the one perfect person presents, people still want to believe that there is something plausible about it. Meanwhile, there were 37% of all people who believed there are a number of possibilities for each of us, but it is our job to go out and find them. A surprising 23% believe that luck is a factor. Psychologists would claim that we create our own so-called "luck." The sooner it seems we abandon the notion of the one ideal, the better we are in getting on with the fun of dating and meeting various people while engaged in our search for a mate.

Superficial Attractions

Women overwhelmingly saw their attraction to men with money as a function of the confidence exuded by these men (83%). Men saw it split between the confidence attraction (54%) and women's desire for material gain (39%). None of the women admitted to an allure of material wealth behind the motivation to date someone with money. This supported an earlier hypothesis about perceptions of men about women and their interest in what a man does for a living, meaning how much money he earns. Still, unless women are lying to us (and possibly themselves), they tell us that while this may be an initial attraction, in the end they date and marry the man who they like the most and fall in love with because of personality and values, not money. Is that similar to man's initial attraction to good looks and subsequent marriage to the woman who makes him feel good about himself and with whom he shares similar beliefs?

Solving Problems

We asked about problem solving strategy. Some may wonder what this has to do with dating and relationships, but I strongly suggest that we tend to resolve problems in our relationships the same way we do in other aspects of our lives. What was interesting to me was the number of people who saw themselves as capable and even responsible for fixing things, no matter what it is. Women had more of a tendency to see themselves as sometimes over-analytical, but by and large, both genders claimed that they believed they can "fix it," no matter what it is (60% of total). It may be that this was a strong indicator of a sense of control and responsibility, in which case, it could be a positive note, or it could mean that people tend to delude themselves. We might be setting ourselves up to fail under this belief, tending to overstay in a relationship because we refuse to give up. We can not fix everything, and nor should we feel that something beyond our control is an admission of failure.

I would have liked to explore this more with these folks. It is possible that the group itself was somewhat biased, by virtue of the fact that those who would participate in a session intended to explore and discuss issues of being single and dating were most likely people who were confident, take-charge types. Therefore this group would more likely respond in a way that exposed their sense of responsibility and control in solving problems. Because so many of them considered themselves "doers" (49% of total), rather than "thinkers," "talkers," or "creators," I have to believe that this assessment is more correct than not.

In spite of all this, however, it turns out that after an evening out when we have had less than a good time, most of us prefer to just leave it alone and avoid the problem, rather than to tell the person. Sixty percent of men and 50% of women said this, compared to 20% of women and only 8% of men who chose to tell their date. The next highest selection from both genders was to thank the date at the end of the evening and "hope" that they do not call again. Perhaps none of us likes rejecting others any more than we enjoy being rejected.

This is another reason behind an appropriate parallel with sales. When we are first with another person, it is true that to some extent, we are selling ourselves to that individual, particularly if we are interested. In sales, we know that there exists some inevitable rejection, and that is why salespeople are often taught that they need to grow a "thick skin." They learn to de-personalize a negative response and perhaps this is a good lesson for all of us. If we didn't take it so personally, if we did not tend to accept someone's disinterest in us as a statement of our worth, we would be less likely to be affected by it. We could simply say well, just as what a salesman sells can not meet the needs of all people, I'm not for everyone.

Besides, in the case of interpersonal relations, we do not want a one-sided arrangement, where we are the one who gives more, or loves more. Here, we need equality. Here, it is imperative that we have a reciprocal arrangement. We needn't settle for less, but of course we do need to convince ourselves of that first, before we are able to convince anyone else.

Passion's Role

The research was consistent with the way in which men and women differ in respect to their thoughts on passion, as well. For men, passion would seem to hold more importance in sustaining a relationship, with 69% of men responding in this way. That is consistent with research that tells us that men rate their wife's ability to make love and the couple's shared interest as the two highest priorities in a marriage, while women said it was more about friends and family ties (confirmed also by a recent Yale Study, reported in the New York Times). Only 30% of females responded this way. While women liked passion, saw it as positive and wonderful, they did not perceive it to be essential to a long-term partnership. Women consistently talk about the value of having a friend, of being able to rely on their mate, to trust him. Still, only about 15% in both genders felt that passion was short-lived, leaving us to consider how most might still believe it could last.

Having had subsequent conversations to clarify the definition of passion, I soon realized that men did not view passion as sex alone. It was part of it, but "passion" was more about the desire to be with someone long-term, and the devotion that comes from knowing, loving and trusting another person. While women had a similar definition for themselves, they tended to believe that men felt passion was more about the physical part of the relationship. This was interesting in light of the research that tells us that men demonstrate their love for a woman physically, while women demonstrate their love more through emotional and verbal expression.

It may have been interesting to explore individual definitions of passion and its impact on a couple. For example, I cannot be entirely certain that the 15% were implying that they believed passion *should* last forever, or if it is truly not unreasonable to suggest that it will or can last forever. One man told me (who did not take the survey and found it interesting that men rated it so highly) that he felt women would be pleasantly surprised at how many men were actually interested in a loving relationship that included only mutually desired and "meaningful" sex.

The Pressure to Commit

Men did seem to feel that a woman pressures them to become serious much before they are ready. One man said, "by the third date, she wants to hear *I Love You*." This comment met with almost complete agreement from the other men in the group, and a discussion then ensued about the difference in perceptions about whether a "date" was in progress or was it merely a casual get together. One man brought up how disturbed he was when a woman would bake cookies for him after only one or two dates. Most men perceived that as a dead giveaway gesture for commitment. This elicited laughter from the group, while one gentleman expressed how this very act by one woman ended up scaring him away also. Other responses were "women want to own you," after a few dates, and he "felt like property" after the third date.

This last discussion disturbed me. I believe that if a man really wants to be with a woman, cookies could never be baked too early and the fact that she expresses a desire to become more serious would never scare him. When we are ready and the person feels good to us (which we know relatively quickly), we aren't likely to perceive advances as negative. I think if these men thought about it, they would find that they had not developed feelings for these women and perhaps even knew that they never would.

Expectations in Communication

Women have expectations that the man should call regularly if he is interested, with about 56% of the women prepared to move on if they haven't heard from the man. Men don't always call to women's satisfaction, and in the early stages of courtship, it isn't even necessarily true that it is due to a lack of interest. Remember how man's earliest experiences taught him autonomy and independence. He needs detachment.

Women were conspicuously silent during this discussion in the focus groups, and not a single questionnaire revealed a similar issue had existed with men toward women. Only 33% of men would be prepared to give up and move on if they had not heard from the woman, with 58% prepared to take action by attempting another contact.

I would not ever want to advocate game-playing in any way, but in some cases, such as with this kind of expectation, it may be better to pretend when the way we really feel is not going to achieve what we would like for the relationship. In other words, if a woman is dying to have this man get serious quickly, she might be better to back off and not act so anxious. This gives the woman time and the man the space he needs.

Particularly when we are in the initial stages of dating someone, such expectation set us up for disappointment and we know that disappointment always leads us to feel victimized. We know that being a victim is something we decide to be, not have to be. In this case, I would rather the woman pretend she has no expectation instead of scaring away someone who might be perfectly wonderful to date had she not been too quick to expose her vulnerability.

Incidentally, our male/female gender distinction with respect to disclosure was corroborated by survey results. A full 70% of people believed that it would be the woman who would be most likely to share the intimate details of her date or relationship. But I thought it was intriguing that there seemed to be a lack of judgment about that, as more men thought it was immaterial (40%) than thought it was bad or wrong. However, only 2% of men thought it was actually "good, because it helped them figure things out," while 42% of women judged it "good" for the same reason.

Taking Action to Meet People

Women and men both expressed some concern in using some of the more modern vehicles to meeting people, such as personals ads and dating services. When looking strictly at numbers via the survey results, it did not seem to be a problem, as we already mentioned. Approximately 39% of the total response indicated that they believed people who use voice personals, for example, were people "a lot like (them)," people who wanted to see what it could add to their lives, and people who were too busy and tired of the other ways on which they had relied.

I did find that those who were most concerned also happened to be least informed, however. For this reason, I would strongly suggest that people who wish to have access to a number of potential prospects but limit themselves due to fear of the unknown become educated on the options. There are enough vehicles to explore and a good amount of information out there to quell our fears, with specific advice on how to remain completely in control and safe while exploring these alternatives.

As we said earlier, the voice personals industry has improved as it has progressed, learning from what surfaced as issues, listening to feedback, and becoming more sensitive to the concerns of its users. The improvements have allowed many more to become actively involved while enjoying the benefits of meeting many more people than they could otherwise.

Sixty-three percent of all respondents rated voice personals ads a 7 or higher on a scale of 1 to 10 with ten being the highest, as a viable option to meeting people to date. Although most, 44%, felt that people would prefer to meet other singles while participating in a mutually enjoyable activity, 57% also felt that personals ads filled a void for those who are too busy and tired of the bar scene. While we did hear some hesitation, 84% of women indicated that using voice personals was "no big deal," while 54% of men indicated the same. Fifty-three percent of women and forty-six percent of men felt that voice personals provided a way for them to control the situation by being able to screen people before deciding to meet them, allowed them access to a large number of candidates that they may otherwise not meet, and meet their need to have this availability in spite of limited time due to busy lives.

Men and women felt similarly about maintaining a lighter tone in writing a voice personals ad, and in what to include and stay away from. They also appeared to have a healthy attitude about being open to the possibilities, yet not having unreasonably high expectations about using the service to meet and date available people.

With respect to specific concerns on using voice personals services, most mentioned cost. It is difficult to comment on that because the user is the one who actually determines cost. Per minute telephone charges are incurred as a result of an individual's decision to stay on the phone. It's really no different than anything else. If it is worth it to us, then it isn't an exorbitant expense when you look at what we might get in the end. If it is not worth it, then we aren't going to do it. Each of us makes the appropriate decision for ourselves when the time comes. Just remember that the individual user manages his or her own search campaign.

Finally, it is a perception issue. We can choose to look at being single and in need of such dating services as an opportunity or as a problem. It really is up to each of us, but it is far better to allow our desire to be our reason for taking action, instead of allowing our fear to hold us back.

A Visually-oriented Society

We asked people whether they felt that we lived in a visually-oriented society, and of course, expected to have that confirmed. While 22% of the women responded that this was "terrible," because good people lose out in this superficial standard, none of the men responded this way. Forty-six percent of the men, in fact, said that this was fine, because beauty is in the eye of the beholder, anyway. A similar percentage, 39% of women responded in this manner. Men and women also responded similarly, 31% and 28% respectively, with regard to not being interested in such people who base their interest in someone on looks alone. Less than one percent in both genders responded that they "had to have" someone good-looking.

I have had dozens of conversations about looks over time with various people and the conclusions are usually the same. No one can deny that in our society good looks has its benefits and rewards. Attractive people get more attention, they get asked out often (as long as they friendlier tendencies and do not intimidate), even are listened to more than people who are less attractive. Of course, we have the billboard models who are held up to us as the ideal, and we all know times when someone good-looking with equal or possibly slightly less qualifications than someone less attractive ends up with the job. We all learn that looks count at a very young age, and since men are visual, they probably feel more strongly about it than women do.

I am not sure that we have anything to feel bad about, as I am relatively confident that this aspect of an individual counts more during the first stages of attraction, and less as we get to know a person. This may say something about finding a way to get to know someone in whom we have interest before we expect them to agree to a date.

What may be the most striking finding, in view of this visual-orientation, is that when asked what people would like to change about themselves, only 14% chose their looks, as opposed to a full 50% who mentioned their level of confidence. First, I guess it would seem that if looks were indeed so important, why wouldn't more of us want to change them, and what does this say about our feelings about who we are? The looks option may simply be reflective of something they feel they can never change, or they may feel that aspect of them isn't truly all that critical. But confidence may be perceived as something that one clearly sees as beneficial and possibly something that can be changed, if only they could figure out how to do it. Confidence is clearly not always a function of how good-looking we are, either; most of us understand this, and it seems clear that most of us want it more than possibly anything else.

It's true that confidence plays a substantial role in getting us a job we want and in the end, and confidence is what gets us noticed by someone we would like to date. This is because when we feel positive about ourselves, others feel positive about us and around us. It is contagious.

I think we already know that no one can give us confidence; that is an aspect of ourselves that we do have the power to improve, but only if we do the necessary work. If we did not get it from our caretakers, then we need to be sure to give it to ourselves. How do we do that? By first believing that we are worthwhile individuals who love ourselves and deserve the love of others, and then to reinforce that by being good to ourselves. We nourish our bodies with good food, adequate sleep, and exercise, we nourish our minds with wholesome input, and we nourish our spirits by trusting our inner guidance to lead us to what is good for us.

Interpretations of Behavior

This surprised me, because when I chose to ask people to interpret someone who touches you (in a non-sexual way), I expected to hear that more people considered touching to indicate an interest in the person. This was not the case. Forty-eight percent of women and 58% of men interpreted "touching" behavior as nothing more than friendliness. When I had asked people informally what they thought was going on between a man and a woman when one touched the other, both men and women seemed to feel it may be more than that. In the survey, more women (38%) actually felt that touching was an indication of interest than men did, with only 25%. This was corroborated in the interviews when women most often said that they would not touch a man for fear he would get the "wrong impression."

This may be an issue of congruency. When we discussed non-verbal communication earlier, we said that body language should not be interpreted in isolation. We needed to see congruent gestures in order to assess the message properly. When I pointed out the behavior to my interviewees, it is possible that they saw more because there was more going on, whereas in the abstract, on paper, we might be more likely to answer the question that is asked without the visual to provide additional cues.

In addition to this feedback, the informal interview sessions I had with single individuals during the previous two years involved those between the ages of 20-something and never married, to 40-something and once or twice married and divorced. The survey did confirm what I had learned in both the informal as well as in-depth interview sessions. Still, I need to mention that very often there is a difference between the way in which one responds who has never been married, to the ones who respond who have been through a failed serious relationship. While the older more experienced may be somewhat wiser, they may also be tainted by history, a bit more circumspect, perhaps even cynical about some aspects of male/female unions.

Attitudes have also changed in the past 20 or 30 years. Being single is acceptable, waiting to marry until the late 30s and 40s, even having children late in life, or choosing not to have children at all is within respected limits. This may account and contribute to the level of calm among the younger people. Then again, they have yet to experience being the odd man out as all their buddies marry before they do.

On Alternative Lifestyles

I am not particularly fond of this expression, although the "*alternatives*" are just as bad. What we are speaking of here, just for the record, are unions, arrangements, other than the "traditional" male/female bond to which I have been addressing myself thus far. So, in an effort to both not offend and to assure an equal amount of respect for the alternative lifestyle, I make this addition.

First, let me say that all the aforementioned still applies to unions of same sex partnerships. There is really only one huge difference and that continues to be in public acceptance. We have come a long way, but we are not there yet. To say that we must be tolerant isn't it, either. Tolerance is really about judging, isn't it? Instead, it is about acceptance, once again, of others and how they are different, not bad, or worse. Change, particularly in the way we think, takes time.

In general, many people are not quite prepared for unconditional acceptance of the reality of this kind of relationship. What I mean by this is that although and perhaps one might "accept" a homosexual couple, they may neither expect them to, nor care for them to be public about it. While that condition wouldn't be held for a heterosexual couple, we hear people say things like, "Well, I don't care what they do behind closed doors -- that's their business -- but do they have to hold hands in public??"

There are two things that need to be said (even as often as they may have already been said). The first, of course, is that there is absolutely no reason to believe that these are bad people or even sad people. The adjectives and descriptives that we put on them are only opinion and judgment; they are our perceptions, nothing more.

Secondly, there is a fair amount of evidence to support the notion that sexual preference is not a *choice*. I mean if we thought about it, who would *choose* a lifestyle in which there was a great potential to be maligned, ridiculed, and in some cases, even persecuted? As I said, many of us are still not 'there,' in terms of complete and unconditional acceptance.

From my own observations, and those that others have reported to me, it seems that gay couples are not at all different from heterosexual ones. Of course, this may be obvious to some, but the interesting thing is how all the information we have discussed thus far applies to these couples. It is believed that the so called "gender war" issues remain intact for the gay couple, as one of the two generally takes on the role of the male in the relationship, and the other takes on the role of the female. In other words, we find that in most gay couple relationships, one is always more expressive of one gender while his or her partner is expressive of the opposite gender.

Although same sex relationships are not the only non-traditional family arrangements, they are probably those that undergo the vast majority of scrutiny. I have even heard so-called religious persons referring to homosexuality as "reprobate," an "abomination," and "evil." They claim that these folks are destined for damnation; they have lost their soul --

God has abandoned them.

It is my personal opinion, and I know of many others, that these accusations are not only false but unwarranted. The God that I have faith in could not have excluded these people on the basis of how they love others. This kind of talk only contributes to an already problematic suicide rate among homosexual persons and continues to pound away at the world's peace.

♥ ♥ ♥

Survey Questions

Here is a sample of the questions we asked singles {They were told that they could check more than one response and that they could also add a response}:

What is/ would be your main motivation for placing a personal ad?

a. that you have someone to do things with {57% men, 63% women}

b. that you don't have to be alone

c. that you add meaning to your existence

d. to establish connection with a potential life partner {43% men, 32% women}

What concerns you most about not having a partner:

a. that people think you're a loser{9% men}

b. that time marches on and you're getting older {25% men, 15% women}

c. that people think you might be gay {8% men, 5% women}

d. feeling alone and lonely {51% men, 55% women}

e. other___________________________________ {7% men, 25% women}

Rank order the importance of the following characteristics in a mate (1-5, with 1 being most important):

Looks 22% men, 5% women personality 43% men, 45% women____Background 9% men, 5% women____ philosophy/values 21% men, 37% women_____Occupation 0% men *% women______

How do /would you decide who to respond to based on a couple of sentences in a personals ad.

a. I look for similar interests 36% men, 50% women

b. I look for romance &% men, 5% women

c. I look for physical attributes that I like 29% men, 9% women

d. I look for creative presentation in the wording {28%men, 31 % women}

When asked out on a first date, women should

a. always pay 0% men

b. never pay 17% men, 45 % women

c. offer to pay 42% men, 30 % women

d. split payment 33% men, 25% women

e. other 8% men

After two people have been regularly dating for a few months, a woman should:

a. Offer to pay 36% men, 43% women

b. never pay 9% men, 19% women

c. split payment 8% men, 5% women

d. take turns paying 47% men, 33% women

What is your opinion on people who use personals ads to find a date:

a. no big deal; it's a viable option {54% men, 84% women}

b. it's okay, but they should keep it a secret because it is embarrassing 0% men

c. you would have to be desperate 0% men)

d. maybe you aren't desperate, but it would look that way {45% men, 16% women}

What is the best thing about being single: Rank your responses (1-4)

a. don't have to answer to or consider anyone else 31% men, 23% women

b. responsible only for self; have a lot less responsibility 13% men, 42% women______

c. time is your own to do whatever you please whenever you please____ 56%men, 29% women

d. other 6% women___________

Who do you think tends to share intimate details of their dates and/or relationships:

Women______80% men 65% women

Men ______11% men 25% women

Neither 9% men, 10 % women

· And you think this is:

a. Immaterial 36% men, 27 % women

b. Good, because it helps them figure things out 27% men, 42% women

c. Bad, because it can sabotage the potential success of the relationship 18% men, 6% women

d. Wrong, because it betrays confidence 19% men, 25% women

Rank these in order of importance in your life (1, highest priority-4, lowest):

a. Satisfying job_____29%men, 32% women

b. Life partner______35% men, 26% women

c. Being a parent_____24% men, 21 % women

d. Having a spiritual presence in life_12%men, 21% women

Do you think most people still hold their first love as a fond memory that can never be upstaged?

Yes_21%men, 16%women_ No_60%men, 42% women____

I don't know___19%men, 32% women___

Do you normally initiate dates and friendships, or do you wait to be approached?

I initiate 19%men, 16% women _____ I wait to be approached 21% men, 26% women_____ It depends_____60%men, 58% women

Which of the following 5 words can be used to best characterizes your disposition

Talker 19% women Doer 37% men, 57%women Thinker 36% men, 24% women Creator 27% men

What is the word that best describes the person you believe is most suited to you?

Talker 17% men, 5% women Doer 42% men, 74% women

Thinker 16% men, 5% women Creator 25% men, 16% women

What do you believe holds the greatest attraction for a couple:

a. to be similar in values and different in temperaments 11% men, 30% women
b. to be similar in values and similar in personality 80% men, 55% women
c. to be different in both values and personality 0% men
d. to think similarly about how to live and raise children 9% men, 15% women

A woman who calls a man:

a. Isn't playing the game right 0% men
b. Appears too anxious and risks losing the man's interest 10% men, 16%women
c. Is a confident, take-charge type woman 46% men, 42% women
d. Scares most men 0% men, 5% women
e. Is unaffected by constraints of society 44% men, 37% women

If you found yourself very attracted to someone on a first date, you would:

a. be frightened into silence/withdrawal 0% men, 5% women
b. take the risk and tell the person 18% men, 32% women
c. pretend to be indifferent and then wait and hope they call again 16% men, 16% women
d. consider it a passing infatuation 0% men, 5% women
e. Want to see the person again and initiate the call 66% men, 42% women

On a first date, you should

a. stay away from personal details about your family 7% men, 5% women
b. not talk too much about an old boyfriend or girlfriend 36% men, 24% women
c. probably not discuss sensitive topics like religion or politics 8% men, 0% women
d. avoid too formal a setting where you would be unable to talk enough to get to know someone 6% men, 14% women
e. all of the above 43% men, 57 % women

After what you determine is a successful first date, you would

a. Expect the person to call soon 33% men, 63% women

b. Call the person if you haven't heard from them within a week or two 50% men, 11% women

c. Wait for them to call and give up after a month 0% men, 5% women

d. Have no expectations 17% men, 21% women

Do you think most people would rather meet

a. through a friend 23% men, 36% women

b. accidentally, a chance meeting 24% men, 18% women

c. at a place where there is an obvious enjoyment of a similar activity (i.e. church group, museum, art gallery, race track) 45% men, 46% women

d. personals ads 8% men

e. computer dating service 0% men

What kind of people do you think use voice personals to find dates?

a. People who are tired of the bar scene 23% men, 45% women

b. People who are too busy to do anything else 24% men, 20% women

c. People who may be desperate 6% men, 0% women

d. People who do not want to date individuals with whom they work 12% men, 0% women

e. All of the above 35% men, 35% women

How would you rate voice personals as a vehicle to meet someone to date?

(Scale of 1-10, with 1 as Low, 10 as High)

1 2 3 4 5 6 7 8 9 10

5 or Below: 19% men, 35% women

6 and Above: 81% men, 65% women

A beautiful, 50 year-old, interesting and intelligent 5'10" woman with a lovely personality has been unattached for 15 years and rarely if ever gets asked out. What's going on?

a. She thinks she is too good for anyone 8% men, 0% women
b. Men are intimidated 21% men, 32 % women
c. She is giving off some sort of negative vibes, or appears unapproachable 58% men, 47 %women
d. Men don't like tall women 7% men, 0%women

Other: 6% men, 21% women

What is your philosophy on dating and meeting a partner

a. There is someone out there for everyone, you just have to find them 44% men, 38% women
b. There is no one perfect, but a number of possibilities in different prospects 37% men, 36% women
c. There is one ideal match waiting out there somewhere 0% men, 0% women
d. It's all luck and happenstance 19% men, 26% women

Do you think it's fair to say that we are a visually oriented society, and how do you feel about that?

a. I think it's okay because beauty is in the eye of the beholder, anyway 46% men, 39% women

b. I think it's terrible, because a lot of people lose out in the superficial process of elimination 0% men, 22% women

c. Who cares, if someone bases their interest in looks alone, I wouldn't be interested in them anyway 31% men, 28% women

d. It's life, and there's nothing we can do about it 15% men, 6% women

e. I have to have a good-looking person 8% men, 5% women

How and when do you know if a date isn't going well?

a. You can't find much to talk about 13% men, 16% women

b. He or she talks way too much about themselves 12% men, 15% women

c. The individual wants to end the evening very early on 18% men, 22% women

d. The person doesn't listen to what you have to say or appears disinterested 19% men, 12% women

e. The person arrives very late with no explanation 0% men, 4% women

f. Any of the above 38% men, 31% women

The reason voice personals appeals to you as a vehicle through which you can meet someone is:

a. because it allows me access to a large audience of potential candidates in a condensed period of time 15% men, 6% women

b. because it provides a way for me to control the situation by screening people before I decide to date them 16% men, 37% women

c. because I am a busy person who just doesn't have the time to meet people 23% men, 5% women

d. all of the above 46% men, 52% women

What does it mean when someone you recently met touches you (not in a sexual way)?

a. That they are just friendly 58% men, 48% women

b. That they have definite interest in you 25% men, 38% women

c. That they are like this with everyone and you are no one special 17% men, 9% women

d. That they're easy 0%men, 5% women

For the most part, men like a good-looking woman because:

a. It's the envy of all the other men who see him with her 25%men, 22% women

b. It's an ego-extension, if he gets her he must be something 38% men, 26% women

c. Men are visual creatures 19% men, 32% women

d. These are the men who cannot make independent decisions; they are operating at a superficial level 6% men, 20% women

e. Other: 12% men

Women like men with money and power because:

a. Power is an aphrodisiac 0% men, 17% women

b. Men like this are accomplished and so carry themselves with a confidence that is attractive to women 54% men, 83% women

c. They want the best things in life and will sacrifice love for material gain 38% men

d. Men without it are useless to women 8% men

What do you need a prospective mate to be good about

a. your family 16% men

b. your friends 15% men

c. your job or profession or ambition 7% men

d. your spiritual beliefs 8% men

e. all of these things 54%men, 100% women

f. none of these because your relationship is only about the two of you 0% men

What is the first thing that attracts you about someone?

a. the way they look 42% men, 18% women

b. the way they smile 21% men, 19% women

c. their personality 22% men, 54% women

d. their intrigue 8% men, 9% women

e. All 7% men

If there were one thing you'd change about yourself, what would it be?

a. my looks 17% men, 12% women
b. my education 8% men, 24% women
c. my confidence level 50% men, 46% women
d. my history 16% men, 18% women
e. Nothing 7% men

How do you tend to solve problems

a. I withdraw from the situation 17% men
b. I get angry and sometimes even violent 0%men
c. I may analyze or over-analyze the situation 0% men, 52% women
d. I have an underlying belief that I can fix it, whatever it is 75% men, 43% women
e. I often expect someone else to solve the problem 0% men, 5% women
f. Other: 8% men

After you have made the decision to place or respond to an ad to meet someone, how would you address that with your children?

a. I tell the children if they are of adolescent age or older 15%men, 17%women
b. I do not tell anyone, including my children, because they do not need to know anyone until it is serious anyway 21%men,44% women
c. I actually involve the children by asking their permission to go ahead with it 14% men, 6% women
d. I only inform the children of the process, but I do not involve them any fur ther in introductions until I feel the person may be a more permanent part of our lives 43% men, 22% women
e. Other: 7% men, 11% women

What are your thoughts on Passion?

a. it's short-lived in most relationships 16% men, 12% women
b. it's what is necessary to sustain a relationship 69% men, 41% women
c. it's only about lust and needs to be de-emphasized 0% men, 0% women
d. it's a creation of the mind; a decision we make 15% men, 18% women
e. Other: 18% women

How many frogs do you think you have to kiss before you find your prince or princess?

a. a lot; there are not a lot of good prospects out there who are unmarried 9% men, 19% women
b. not many because there are many potential princes and princesses 33% men, 25% women
c. too many; that's why I'm trying to save myself time with voice personals 9% men, 0% women
d. Even if the number is many, it's fun; it all depends on how you look at it! 42% men, 56% women
e. Other: 7% men

If you don't hear from someone you've dated once after two weeks, do you

a. call them 59% men, 33% women
b. continue to wait for them to call 0% men, 6% women
c. forget about them and move on 33% men, 56% women
d. tend to get down and experience difficulty overcoming the disappointment 8% men, 5% women

What do you say at the end of an evening when it has not been a good date?

a. thank them and hope they don't call again 17% men, 21% women

b. thank them and let them know that it is not going to happen again 9% men, 20% women

c. leave it alone and just not answer their calls in the future 41% men, 5% women

d. leave it alone for the moment and wait to reject them over the phone 25% men, 35% women

e. Nothing, then afterwards I'm always busy when they call 8% men, 19% women

Do you think most people prefer feeling love for the person before having sex with them?

a. women do, because most women have trouble separating the physical act from the emotional connection 8% men, 20% women

b. men do not care as much because men are more physical and can separate the two 16% men, 19% women

c. both men and women prefer it, but men are less likely to require it 54% men, 33% women

d. both men and women possess the animal instinct that drives them but it is their sense of decency, morality, and need for commitment that sets boundaries and prevents it from happening 15% men, 28% women

e. Other: 7% men

What type of people can you expect to meet through voice personals:

a. Lazy people 0% men, 0% women
b. People a lot like me, with similar motivations for pursuing this option 25% men, 47% women
c. Desperate people 0% men, 0% women
d. People interested in testing the waters and having some fun with it 17% men, 29% women
e. All of the Above 58% men, 24% women

What are your personal expectations once you agree to meet someone face-to-face, after speaking to them over the phone via voice personal ad?

a. High expectations because I have done a good job screening them on the phone and feel I rather know them by date time 14% men, 5% women
b. I expect little to nothing because I do not wish to set myself up for disappointment 21% men, 6% women
c. I go in with no great expectations but open to whatever happens 36% men,62% women
d. I figure that at the very least, I could end up meeting an interesting person 22% men, 29% women
e. All I want is one good and pleasant evening out 7% men, 4% women

When writing a personals ad, one should (Rank order these 1-4 in order of importance)

a. stay away from giving out information that is too personal, such as number of children, ages of children, etc. 0% men, 17% women
b. never include any sexual content 33% men, 26% women
c. avoid any reference to long-term goals, such as marriage, etc. 9% men, 23% women
d. maintain a lighter tone, avoiding any content too serious for a public ad 50% men, 34% women
e. Other: 8% men

Is there anything else you need to tell us/ anything we should know about being single and dating????

♥ ♥ ♥

DateNotes

- Study findings are intended to raise awareness and help us by giving us ideas on how others have resolved problems similar to those we experience. Usually we find that we are not alone in our feelings and thoughts. Although our issues can look very much alike, we may have such unique ways of responding to them. Keep learning from others. Read, talk to other people, listen well.

- There's an old saying about the only two rules you need in life: The first rule is, *Don't sweat the small stuff.* The second rule is, *(Realize that) it's all small stuff.* Make peace of mind your only goal, especially when it comes to relationships.

- Please don't let things like money or good looks get in the way of your happiness. Even if you had more of either or both, it wouldn't be any guarantee, and people who have them can tell many stories where those "assets" have actually gotten in their way on occasion. Be convinced that you have something no one else does, and it has nothing at all to do with money or good looks.

- If you did have everything you thought you needed to make a good impression, such as money, power, *and* good looks, how would you know that someone loves you for *you*?

- Expectations can be dangerous because they often result in our disappointment. When we feel disappointed, we also tend to feel victimized and this places us in a weak position as we feel lacking in control of our lives. That's unnecessary, as we do have control once we take responsibility.

Nine

PRACTICAL MATTERS

The last of the human freedoms—to choose one's attitude in any given set of circumstances, to choose one's own way.
Viktor Frankl

Whether we are only thinking of taking advantage of the various vehicles to begin meeting new people, or we've already met someone, it behooves us to be acquainted with a few particular practical matters.

A first date

There is a play running on Broadway entitled, "I Love You, You're Perfect, Now Change." In it, a first date is depicted. The anxiety is so high between the two people involved that they decide that it is too much pressure, talk each other into a second date, walk a few steps away from one another and return to proceed with date number two. Most of us know what that's like. We would love to be able to skip right over that initial awkwardness that accompanies our first meeting and get directly to the date which occurs after we have already decided that it is good enough to pursue. Unfortunately, we do not have that impractical option like the people in the show. We have to experience the anxiety, and sometimes we experience it so often, we actually get good at it.

Some things to consider on the first date:

- Wear something appropriate to the occasion. If you are completely unsure, ask your date what might be appropriate.

• If you need to suggest a place to go, recommend something moderately priced, especially if your date expects to pay.

• Be yourself, although you will automatically be your best self, especially if there is immediate chemistry.

• Be confident and smile. Remember how important that smile is in conveying acceptance of another.

• Use your date's name often. People like to hear their name and it's a good "sales" technique.

• In your conversation, make every attempt to listen intently. You might ask questions that relate to what they talked about. You might even repeat things they have said, reinforcing your attentiveness and making him or her feel important.

• Do not look at other women or men while you are with your date. It is rude.

• Do not speak of old boyfriends or girlfriends except if asked, and do not go into detail.

• Maintain a balance between talking and listening. Remember to ask your date questions if you feel you are talking too much.

• Do not order food that could be difficult to manage.

• Do not fabricate or exaggerate.

• Compliment your date, but only when sincere, and be specific.

• Finally, be honest about "next time." If you would like to see them again, go ahead and mention something about hoping that the two of you will have an opportunity to discuss or to do this again. If you have no intentions, either remain quiet or decline the offer kindly.

How to know When the Date's in Trouble...

Your date can't stop talking about his/her former love interest. While it can be nothing more than a basic case of nerves, it does not bode well for receptivity toward a new love interest when one continues to look back to the past.

Sometimes people do this without even realizing it. It is best not to get angry or to retaliate with stories of your old flames. You might want to ask questions, listening to what is being said in getting to know the person. What are they telling you about themselves? This can prove to be a very revealing scenario if you aren't too easily threatened.

Your date appears very interested in and concerned with who is looking as you both enter a room. Preoccupation with what is happening around the dating scene might suggest that there is some agenda for having asked you out. Such antics are questionable, since any agenda other than interest in you on a date is unacceptable. No matter how complimented you may be tempted to feel, don't ever rationalize or be willing to be used as a pawn in anyone's hidden agenda. You deserve undivided attention.

There are possibilities for this behavior. The one inferred above is to impress someone or cause someone else to be jealous. The other is related, but suggests that you are being used as an ornament to decorate your date's arm. And finally, it may be that this is simply someone who has problems with jealousy, bothered by anyone looking at their date. If the date lasts beyond the initial entry, try to get the individual to be comfortable and ask them what the problem is. It may be an opportunity to have a heart-to-heart discussion.

*Wherever you go, your date is busy looking around; eyes are rarely on you...*even when you are supposed to be engaged in conversation. Eye contact demonstrates interest, sincerity, and plain respect for the other individual. If you can't achieve undivided attention on a first date, it's likely you never will.

Again, reasons for this behavior can vary, but it is difficult for us not to take offense when someone who is supposedly interested in us acts like they are having an attention deficit problem. If you really like this person, you may want to try levity, ask them what they are looking for, and stop talking when they are not attending. Resume when they return the courtesy to you.

He or she uses language like, "you should," "you have to," "you're supposed to." This can mean serious judgment and conditional acceptance of you as a partner, or even as a friend. No one needs this kind of judgment and each of us deserves unconditional love and acceptance.

On another level, while everyone wants to be respected and accepted for exactly who they are, no one really cares to be held up to such a high standard, one that even the best of us feel challenged by and unable to meet. Not meeting a standard usually either causes us to internalize and self-blame or externalize, taking blame out on the world around us. There is nothing wrong with calling someone on their choice of words. Remember, they are most likely harder on themselves than they are on you.

Other cues of disinterest include inconsistent attention from the individual, someone who never returns a compliment, and someone who declines your offer to get together more than two consecutive times. If all advances are one-sided, or you suspect someone is being less than honest, it is probably wise to let it go now instead of investing any additional time and energy in the relationship.

How to Know If Someone Loves You

The three magic words. Some people place too much emphasis on hearing the words, "I love you." Others feel that they never need to say it; they *show* it, that ought to be enough. Still others have a great deal of trouble with serious verbal disclosure; they are uncomfortable, feel it is tantamount to exposing their vulnerabilities. Finally there are a few who say it frequently enough, sometimes too frequently, that it's almost perfunctory or a matter of habit. The motive is to comply when someone needs to hear it, so the words are rendered meaningless.

Saying "I love you" is not something that can be choreographed. We are usually quite adept at distinguishing between sincerity and obligation, anyway. Truthfully, none of us wants to either say or hear these words unless they are truly meant.

So it isn't about the words. What is it then? Here are a few things to think about:

LISTENING

When you're with the person you love, do you feel like he or she is *with you*? Absence does not need to be physical. Emotional absence is dreadful and hurtful to the person we are with. Think of the couples you see out to dinner with no conversation taking place. That kind of distance is unreachable.

When two people sincerely love one another, they not only hear what the other says, but they listen and are interested in what the other has to say. Even if they do not agree, their thoughts and feelings are not dismissed.

We discussed the value of good listening earlier and all of it applies here as well. Even if we need to practice this as a skill, it makes good sense because it tells the person we love that they are important, valued, and appreciated. Listening skills include the eye contact and mirroring what was said, if that is necessary. It will not go unnoticed.

SUBTLETY

Soft touches: hand across your back as he opens a door, looks into your eyes when he speaks to you, even if there are others present.

She touches your arm, leg, your face, as she speaks and looks into your eyes.

Subtlety says so much about care and tenderness felt toward another. I remember hearing someone say that she loved being kissed on the forehead. That's it; a kiss on the forehead is so different than a kiss on the mouth.

Eye contact is important, much is told with the eyes alone. If your partner has it with you, you may go ahead and interpret this as positively as you wish. Body language experts say that if someone holds eye contact with you for longer than a 20-second interval, you may take it personally!

CONSIDERATION

He or she considers you and your feelings about or on something. This means that we do not make commitments without the other person, and we respect our partner's privacy and opinions, even when we do not agree.

We ought to feel 100% respected. We all know what this feels like. When we are respected, we feel positive, it enhances our self-esteem. When we are not respected, our self-esteem is compromised.

DISAGREEMENTS ARE NOT ATTACKS

Learn how to manage conflict or an argument. There is a technique: Face each other, look into one another's eyes, and express yourself in terms of *your* feelings ... rather than use language of attack.

Some ground rules apply:

- Use 'Me language instead' of 'You language'
- Calm down before you approach the discussion.
- Assume the belief that you'd rather be happy than right.

Bear in mind that when we argue, it is rarely about what we think (and say) we're arguing about. Ask yourself to answer the question honestly, first to yourself (what is this, really?), before you can be honest with your partner. You will both benefit from the conscious awareness.

Fighting can be a form of intimacy if we do it well. After all, we often hear of all the fun people have making up. But we do need to know how to fight, as there is a good way and a bad way to do it. Raising our voices may be more about the need to be right and probably is a bad way. Discussion, instead, while it may be intense, usually takes place after we have calmed down, allowing for real listening and empathy.

Arguing with another tells them that they are wrong. In other words, it is an attack of the person. When we attack someone, we cause defensive reactions. That's never a productive encounter. Again, we need to understand that we won't always and don't always have to agree.

APPRECIATION

So many people speak of the importance of feeling appreciated. That's because when we feel unappreciated, we tend to feel undervalued, sometimes taken for granted and not cared for. This is important to us when we are in a relationship. We all want and need to feel that someone knows we are there, and that our presence matters.

REASONABLE AGE...
IS THERE A "RIGHT" AGE TO MARRY?

We might be able to talk about this one "right." At least it's closer to being a reality ... the right time to marry, as opposed to any other 'right!'

Have fun, go to school, travel, see many people. That is sound, practical advice. Form male and female friendships. Be sure to get to know/love you before inviting someone into your too young, rather immature, and not-quite-wise-enough-yet life. This is good advice, but we will all go about our decisions with unique philosophies and sense of what is right *for us*.

Probably the best time to settle down is age 30. By then, we will have gotten to know ourselves and have kissed enough frogs to understand what we want and need. Spend a couple or few years getting to know each other by living together before you begin having children. Offspring will never make a weak marriage stronger and children do not deserve to come into a home where there is questionable love.

HOW TO KNOW IF YOU ARE "MARRIAGE MATERIAL"

Get married, in any case. If you happen to get a good mate, you will be happy; if a bad one, you will become philosophical, which is a fine thing in itself.

Socrates (d. 399 B.C.,) in Diogenes Laertius, Lives.

We can love someone and not be faithful, but that's not part of the marital deal as we are legally bound. I have spoken to a number of married men who admit to not being faithful to their vows. They do not appear to be the least bit anxious about it, short of getting caught, and really have no intention of divorcing their spouse. They seem to feel entitled to a mistress outside the marriage. Reasons? Among them, the yearning for passion, the fact that they perceive their wives to be too busy with the children, leaving no time for them, sheer availability and opportunity.

A good clue that you are *not* marriage material, at least for the moment, is if you have a need to be with more than one person, play the field, sow your oats. If you've not yet made one big decision for yourself, do not let marriage be the first. Do something, like go away to school, or get a job while you are getting an education, select a career, develop a lifestyle. Spend time figuring out who you are before you go and decide who you want.

Until you feel that you are mature enough to make such a serious decision, have done your desired share of dating, and have considered this person you wish to marry to be a lifetime partner, do *not* do it! This is not to deny the possibility that sometimes things go wrong and divorce is the only answer, but it is to caution against having the attitude that divorce is always an alternative *upon entering* a commitment.

WHAT ABOUT KIDS...?

Having children, with only few exceptions, should never be considered before you graduate from high school, and probably not even until after college. We are simply not equipped to handle such a serious lifestyle change and commitment while we are still becoming who we are going to be.

And here's the thing...if you really want to test the waters on having children, don't get pregnant, get a pet—preferably one with a fairly regular maintenance requirement, such as a dog, even a cat. If after you have had a pet and been successful keeping it fed, clean, and picked up after, if you have been adequately responsive and responsible in caring for it, arranging care for it in your unavoidable absence, been patient with its urgings, generous with your time in loving and hugging your pet, then perhaps you may well consider a child. But not one second before that!

"ENDING IT"

When it comes to breaking off with someone, it does help to have some idea of what we should do and what we probably need to avoid doing. One woman brought me back to the job analogy when she said that it's like when you know the writing is on the wall because the company is cutting back. You try to beat them to the punch by getting out before they ask you to leave. When a relationship is going bad, she said, you try to get out before the other one does.

I recently spoke to a gentleman who said that if people knew how to break up a relationship, they wouldn't be so afraid to begin one. I thought those were two interesting perspectives. We do have normal fear about being abandoned, and about uncertainty. And we do have fears about being hated and of hurting someone. So it is perhaps true that we may scare ourselves out of even starting something.

Incidentally, the man went on to explain how his thoughtful teen-age son wrote a very nice letter to a girl whom he had been seeing, telling her in a frank, sincere way that they would not date any longer, taking responsibility for the reasons he knew it could never work. In other words, he was completely honest and straightforward, but careful not to injure her self-esteem in anyway. He was proud of his son and I thought how nice it was to have someone so young be that sensitive and caring about another human being.

We might think of how we would like for someone to end it with us, but here are some tips that may be useful when you no longer wish to see someone:

- Do not tell the person over the phone or immediately preceding a holiday
- Do not say mean things—you'll feel badly afterwards and so will they
- Do not be disingenuous with your reasons—say only what is truthful regarding your desire to end it
- Don't let guilt talk you out of it
- Do not begin discussing or blaming the person for what they did or did not do—there is no need to hurt the person in any additional way
- Be respectful, allow the other person to deal with the bad news in their way
- Try to put it in terms of how it is best for both of you
- Say something nice –there must be some reason you originally wanted to date this person. Boosting their self-esteem will help, but only if it is sincere
- Take responsibility and express that to the person
- Be specific and firm about what you want to have happen. Being vague leaves room for misinterpretation. It'll only be confusing and possibly cause someone to have false hopes.

THE SINGLE PARENT

Single parents have even greater demands and stresses to contend with in the dating arena. Any interest in someone has to involve and include consideration of the children. For mothers, it may mean that they are working outside the home, trying to balance the needs there with those of her job. We all know that the superwoman concept is a myth. Something inevitably suffers. Women are doing their best to live up to a modern ideal and may be paying a heavy price. When they are at work, they worry about their children and feel guilty about all the time they spend away from them. When at home, they feel guilty that they are not able to give one hundred percent to their work. If we are physically at one place and emotionally at another, how can we ever be fully present *where we are, in the moment?* As we try desperately to live up to what society dictates is the 'thoroughly modern woman,' we may lose who we truly are in the process.

It's easy to understand how single parents have additional concerns about dating. Although they may be very interested, they understand that they cannot get involved with someone in a vacuum. With time passing so quickly, both men and women recognize that they aren't getting any younger, and they'd at least like to be able to entertain the idea of dating while raising their children. Parents shouldn't have to completely put their personal lives on hold. Having children doesn't have to mean that we cannot date or that if we do, it must only be done under certain circumstances.

Part of being good to and for our children means setting positive examples and being content in our own lives. If we'd bc happier with a partner, then we need to progress toward that goal to ensure that we are the best that we can be for our children. Like all of us, however, single parents are best to get their personal situations in order before they decide to get actively involved in dating.

Children want their parents to be happy, so it shouldn't be all that difficult to have a discussion to inform them of our intentions. We do have a responsibility, however, to make wise choices in who we decide to introduce into our family and when the appropriate time is for that introduction to occur. We do not want to be premature, as we know that children can become easily attached and then subsequently hurt in the event of a brief liaison.

COMMON MISTAKES [before "I do"]

1. **"Free Milk" - Why should he buy the cow...?**

Good question. Old and odd question. Usable, however. Practical, even.

About sex on dates:

As already mentioned, we need to get to know the person before we can tell whether it is a worthwhile relationship. Don't waste love on sex. It's not the same. Can't be. It never *will* be.

In the age of AIDS, people still have sex indiscriminately; in an era of abundantly available birth control, people continue to do it without contraception. And at a time when the old double standards persist amidst advancements in perceptions, people have sex on impulse, giving in to instincts and hormones and the influence of mind-altering substances. So, we need to talk about it. It seems we cannot talk *enough* about it to get people to think before they act.

It is a rare man who thinks well of the woman who sleeps with him on a first date. What a woman thinks of a man who *asks* on a first date is probably not quite as negative. It may be more expected and even accepted. Some cultural double standards die hard and slow. This one hasn't moved much in my lifetime from my perspective.

Of course, women are not cows, and men certainly do not need to "buy" them. Still, having self-respect and understanding our right to say no (without the fear of loss) is ideally the baseline from which all women should operate.

2. **Settling for Okay, Good Enough,**

OR just Second Best

I once worked with a woman who constantly complained about her marriage. Whenever anyone would question her about getting a divorce, she would insist that she wouldn't even think of it,... until she "found someone else." She meant someone *better*. Someone, but not just anyone, and he probably would have *money*, "this time." She refused to be alone, as she was just about 30 years of age.

Usually, when I hear this kind of talk from women I think of the goldigger reputation. For this particular lady, it probably wouldn't have been a bad idea for her to spend some time alone getting herself together, instead of going from one relationship directly into another. But she did end up leaving her husband, and she did wait until she had met someone else. She soon married the new man, who was from a well-to-do family, and although her first husband was initially crushed, he ultimately met someone also. Both presently have children and seem happy with the outcome.

Whenever we feel as though we are settling, it can never be a good thing. It's no more acceptable for us to do this to another than it is to do it to ourselves. We both deserve better, deserve to be loved wholly. But people do settle for a number of reasons, not the least of which is their age and children. Rather than feel you must 'settle,' try something to open up the possibilities, like meeting a number of different people from news ads or dating services. That way you get to at least have a better idea of who you might want, and better, who you are inside a relationship.

A Complaint AFTER **"I DO"**

Sex: quality and frequency:

Some men say that all their wives wanted was the children; they feel left out and neglected. Some justify extra-marital sex and /or relationships because of this perceived neglect.

People do not suddenly stop wanting sex. At least not without some kind of physical reason. The fact is that by the time someone begins not having sex physically, that person has likely stopped wanting and enjoying sex emotionally some time before. Like it or not, this is a two way street.

Here again, the complaints may end up being similar from the perspectives of both genders. It is usually a concern of quality. Especially after marriage, it is important to attend to the details of expressing our love physically. While some may be thinking this is because it can get very boring, I hope the majority of us understand the real reason behind making the effort. Monogamous lovemaking can be one of the most satisfying intimate experiences. We ought to be using it to grow in our intimate connections and reach the height of experience to which we were fully intended.

Relationship experts have reported that the majority of women want to know how they can get more love and affection *outside* the bedroom. In other words, there is an obvious "adequate" amount of sexual activity, but a dearth of what women need to feel loved. What that means, men, is that women don't feel automatically loved by what goes on in the bedroom; they need something else. Something as simple as the subtle gestures of a touch, a kiss on the cheek or the forehead, kindness, expressions of appreciation.

Men, these same experts claim, have a greater preoccupation with whether the passion in their relationship can last. My inclination is to throw this question directly back at the asker--that is, what will you do to ensure that passion remains? If you do nothing, then you simply cannot expect too much. An ounce of prevention is truly worth a pound of cure as the procrastinating silent resentment and repression will only cause you to act in an unadmirable way.

WE MIGHT WANT TO CONSIDER THE ADVANTAGES OF BEING SINGLE:

What you don't need a partner for:

- *To eat*: You may eat WHAT, WHEN, and WHERE and HOW you

wish to...

- *To attend social functions*: As an individual, you would attend a function without having to be concerned with someone else having a "good time."
- *To sleep with*: You may read in bed until whatever time you please; you needn't be concerned about being awaken by someone else's nightmares or noises, or awakening them.
- *To go to the movies*: who cares, once the lights go out, you don't want to talk to anyone anyway.
- *To shop*: It is difficult to understand even wanting to go shopping with someone else, if in fact there is a purpose to your trip. The only way it makes sense is if you have no particular agenda and you make it a social event. Otherwise, when you need to be productive, you also need to be alone.
- *To have a baby*: Nowadays, we know that there are sperm banks and egg donors. If you truly desire to be a single parent, it is entirely possible. Just so long as you do it for reasons of sharing unconditional love and not pure selfish reasons. And please remember that the ideal situation for any baby to be brought into this world is with a man and woman who are devoted to one another and to the care and concern for the human being they together created.
- *To love yourself*: This is the *most* important. You do *not* need one single other person to love yourself unconditionally. You can choose to do that *right this minute and for all time.*

Actually, there isn't much we *need* another person for. Obviously, we may be more comfortable having someone else to pal around with at the movies, etc.. Nevertheless, we need to know and understand that it is never a matter of necessity.

Applying the "be-do-have" theory *...as a final practical matter...*

As mentioned in a previous chapter, we usually set goals by deciding what we WANT. Then we go and get what we believe we need to accomplish our objectives so that we *have* all the things necessary to *do* whatever we want to be doing. Then we do it. After a while, I guess we feel if we continue the doing long enough, we must *be* whatever it is we set out to be.

Only that's not the way it works. Often what we find when we approach our goals in this backward manner is that we never FEEL quite like we think we are supposed to. We might *have* the "stuff," we *do* the "thing," but somehow we continue to lack the inner sense that we ARE what we have been aspiring toward. This is because unless it happens first in our head, the self image part, all that we do will feel like nothing more than activity. We can not confuse activity with accomplishment.

We must always first be what we want to be in our minds. It must be part of our own self image, the picture we have of ourselves. Then, we will *do* the things that people who have similar goals do, until we finally *have* the things that those people have.

Translating this theory into practice in the case of a "search" for a life partner, we first must be who we are with personality, desires, needs, etc. This assumes that we are in touch with what that is in ourselves. Because we are that particular way, we would naturally begin to do the things that people similar to us in goals and values would do. Finally, after we have been doing what we are for a while, it follows that we would have the things that make sense to have, given who we are.

This is a critical distinction in goal setting. It applies generally, of course, but in this book we are speaking of a life mate. So that I decide I am an individual with a positive self image. I like myself and I realize that I alone am responsible for my individual happiness. This means that my actions and behavior are consistent with individuals who likewise have a positive self esteem and image. I am naturally attracting and attracted to the same kinds of positive people. It follows then that I have the things, lifestyle, etc., that these folks have. That is how we achieve goals.

No mate can ever help us get to where we want to be if we do not possess that in and of ourselves. And no amount of having and doing will get us being what and where we want without having first begun within ourselves.

So, be who you are, you will naturally do what you do because of who you are, and the having—the certain someone who meets with those dominant thoughts and behaviors which you naturally exhibit—will come, most likely without you having to do one intentional thing to get them there.

♥ ♥ ♥

DateNotes

- We can't always be "practical." Because we are so often governed by our subconscious, we do things and say things we wish we hadn't. But just because you did something in the past, does n't mean that you couldn't change what you do in a similar situation going forward.

- We won't always listen, either. Just because someone gives advice doesn't mean that it will work for us, does it? The most logical thing to do would be to think of advice as additional information that might be assimilated into the repertoire of knowledge that you've already built through experience. And then, let intuition be your guide. If you really listen, you'll actually "hear" your heart talk to you. It is the least fallible of all our guidance sources.

- It would be better if we had laws for things like youngest age allowable to marry and have children, a pass/fail test for parent ing and for whether we are ready for that level of commitment. But, we don't. The decision is ours, and we need to self-impose strict guidelines that reflect the most honest assessment of our individual readiness.

- Don't settle, and don't get pressured into situations that you would not want your best friend to be subjected to. This isn't a dress rehearsal, it's the real thing, and as far as we know, it's our only chance. Do not do or stay in places that do not add to your life. When we act in a self-preserving way, remember that we save at least two people from potential heartache.

Ten

THE RELATIONSHIP

...Relatedness means staying in life, even when it becomes complicated and when meaning and clarity are elusive. It means living with the particular individuals who come into our lives, and not with our ideals and images of the perfect mate...The soul wants to be attached, involved, and even stuck, because it is through such intimacy that it is nourished, initiated, and deepened.

Thomas Moore, *SoulMates* (1994)

Best Advice For A Long Lasting Relationship

and...What I Want In A Man/ Woman:

If you're one of those persons who has taken to writing a list of characteristics or demands on what you are seeking in a life partner-- particularly at the insistence of so-called relationship "experts,"-- let me only say that you'd be best advised to tear up that list and start over with a list entitled "WHAT I WANT IN AND FOR MYSELF." It will never be about another person before it is about you.

In conducting the research for dating and relationship advice, I came across the original version of Dale Carnegie's *How To Win Friends and Influence People.* In this 1936 copyright edition, Mr. Carnegie provides us with seven rules for creating a happy home life. The more I read, the more I saw how his work demonstrated that meeting someone we want to have a relationship with is not a matter of chance, luck, or being at the right time or right place. It is about creating the relationship we want once we are ready for that kind of commitment. I think that the reason many of us fail is not because we are with the wrong person so much as we were just not ready. This readiness factor gets us right back to the work we need to complete on ourselves first before we become a couple. And that same readiness allows us the attitude and motivation to create the life we want.

Here are the original thoughts of Dale Carnegie, whose book and material continues to inspire people all over the world:

- *Don't nag* (Chapter: "How To Dig Your Marital Grave in the Quickest Possible Way")
- *Don't try to make your partner over* (Chapter: "Live and Let Live")
- *Don't criticize* (Chapter "Do This and You'll Be Looking Up the Time-Tables to Reno")
- *Give honest appreciation* (Chapter: "A Quick Way to Make Everybody Happy")
- *Pay little attentions* (to your partner) (Chapter: "They Mean So Much to a Woman") —remember, this was a long time ago
- *Be courteous* (Chapter: "If You Want to Be Happy, Don't Neglect This One")
- *Read a good book on the sexual side of marriage* (Chapter: "Don't Be a Marriage Illiterate")

I found this material interesting in light of the fact that it represented and continues to capture the essence of what is important in any long-term relationship today. I could not have summarized what I had heard and read any better than Carnegie did way back then. And these points are just as applicable in dating *and,* of course, in winning friends!

In a relationship, it is important to be friends. The most successful marriages aren't those that never argue, they aren't even necessarily those that begin at ages of maturity, but they always have the element of friendship contained within their relationship. That means they like each other, they afford one another the kindness and concern that all of us do to friends with whom we wish to maintain a long-term relationship.

"I am looking for the right combination: intellect, but not arrogant, beauty but not conceit, personality, charm, wit, etc, etc." This sort of thinking can be a trap both to being what will eventually be labeled 'too picky,' and to keep our attention diverted away from our own issues --the stuff we have to address before we invite someone into our lives.

Married Folks I have known...

What seems to work, What does not

Just like everyone else, I have seen my share of good, bad and mediocre marriages. First, let's look at marriages that none of us really want. Here are some of the tell tale signs of THE BAD, or

The "Unconscious Marriage":

- Going through the motions; you are not friends.
- You feel like he only eats and sleeps at your house.
- You feel like all she ever wanted from you is to have children. Since then, you've served your purpose, she is "finished" with you.
- You don't laugh together (anymore).
- You have nothing to talk about at the dinner table.
- You are together "for the kids."

- You have stopped caring one way or the other; you're apathetic.
- When you are out, it's always with other people.
- You rarely have a night out together. Neither of you initiates.
- Sex is an act. There is no emotion in it.
- Arguments end up in defensive reactions or withdrawing of emotion

The Good, or "Passionate Friends":

The thriving marriages I have witnessed have contained these characteristics:

- They seem like close friends, often laughing together and openly expressing signs of affection.
- Demonstrate genuine interest in each other's lives.
- They seem to discuss, never yell. The discussion is open and honest, with few, if any secrets.
- When disciplining their children, they speak with one voice. If they differ, it is discussed in private.
- They are supportive of each other's career goals, aspirations, and separate interests.
- They speak (well) of the other when in public situations.
- They often share memories of when they first met or another sweet occasion.
- They are kind, cordial, and considerate of members on both sides of the family.
- They appear to view their "differences" in a way that makes their marriage more exciting-- not painful—there is a lack of contempt or insults.

- They are respectful of one another and kind to the parent(s) of the other.
- Criticism is limited to expressions in I versus You language
- They praise one another and let one another know how they understand them.

♥ ♥ ♥

DateNotes

- ♥ When people are happy in a relationship, it usually has something to do with working from a base of friendship.
- ♥ They are normally intimate in verbal expression as well as in the bedroom.
- ♥ They tend to make the attempt to understand the other's point of view, even if they continue to differ.
- ♥ When they fight, they do not attack, rather accept responsibility for their part and deal with (rather than hide) negative emotions.
- ♥ They trust each other.
- ♥ They enjoy interests that they share in common, yet maintain (and allow for) separate ones.
- ♥ They are flexible when they need to change for the sake of the relationship and tolerant of change in their partner.

Eleven

DEEPER MATTERS

The great tragedy of life is not that men perish,
but that they cease to love.
W.Somerset Maugham

Ceasing to Love

I think of all the saddest things about loving is the notion that we give up. We settle, or we don't believe what we once believed about love. It was a fairytale. We were hoodwinked. Now, we're realists. We either can't, don't, or won't believe in the notion of true love, soul mate, lifelong marriage partner.

While it is obvious that I am not one to believe in a one perfect person theory, I very definitely believe that we come here specifically to meet certain people. Some we know for a day, perhaps only a passing moment -- others for somewhat longer, and some for a lifetime. All relationships have meaning in our lives; they are all to teach us. If we remain open to the experience, we invite others to share in our purpose here. Going through life with someone, and joined by as many as we contact along our journey, allows us all the joy to which we are entitled.

Buying in to cultural ideals and stereotypes is sure to lead us down an unnecessary path of a not-so-positive learning experience. No one can dictate to another what "should" be, or what is universally nice, good, or great. We need not feel that we are here to either live up to some expectation, nor to please someone at the expense of our own self-esteem. You alone can describe your needs most accurately, and as unique as that will be, you have every right to be proud and excited by that uniqueness. There will never be another like you; there was never any need to have a second one, as you were perfect the first time. But it is not that anyone can tell you this. You must believe it first in your own heart. The rest, I assure you, will fall into place.

All the negative feelings you will ever have about relationships can be reduced to the common denominator of fear. Fear is at the base of all negative emotion. Whether you feel guilt or frustration or anger or resentment or even loneliness, it is because you are experiencing fear. Learn to be quiet with yourself to figure out just what your soul is trying to tell you. It will not only reveal the cause of the fear, but it will provide you with the answer. The only thing you need to do is be quiet and listen ... and believe.

My father used to say that you can always predict a man's behavior with his wife by observing his parents and the way he interacts with them. Probably just because my father had four daughters and only one son did he have an interest in driving this point home. I suspect it can go either way. That is, a woman's behavior in a romantic union may be predicated at least to some extent, on her relations with her parents. The point is that we all come from a certain background, a lifestyle that most likely had a good deal to do with our thoughts, attitudes, how we believe, and ultimately behave.

We will undoubtedly use our earliest role models in directing similar emotions to our love relationships. While we can see changes in people, it is usually not without some degree of hard work and it will always be accompanied by a sincere desire on the part of the person wishing to change. We do need to examine a prospective partner's relationship with his parents. It is a good gauge of at least what we might expect of their potential. Once we love him or her, acceptance and 100% unconditional love is the only gift we'll ever need to give them. And the one that they will treasure for a lifetime.

Truth or Illusion?

It seems the biggest issue that we continually grapple with comes down to two fundamental premises. They are the world of truth or the world of illusion. The former is what we are in perpetual search of, the latter is what we usually live with.

We have already said that fear is false evidence appearing real. And we have identified all negative emotion as fear manifest. So, the negativity with which we live seems all to be a result of some false input. It is illusory because we have made it up. We thought it was real because we hurt and cry and feel bad.

What we often fail to recognize is that we are simply perpetuating negative emotion in our lives by lending credence to it. In other words, we believe that it is. But this is only because we made up the belief in the first place.

It is our birthright to have truth's revelations in our lives. That means that we have both the capability and the responsibility to have truth manifest during our time here, on our earthly learning expedition. Truth, while somewhat unique for each of us, begins with the fundamental fact that we are here for a visit. Life as we know it is an experience from which we learn many valuable things, and after which we will return to a common home. This is the place where we have the experiences and make the choices that make our lives happy or not.

Now, if this sounds a little too spiritual for you, it's okay. You may teach me something. I believe for all the studying I have done, both in "real life" and in books, this is about as perfect an explanation as I can offer. It works for me.

And so what does the truth or illusion theory have to do with meeting our 'perfect' mate? Everything. Depending on how we approach life, and specifically our ideas about the one most important relationship we will have during our earthly experience, will determine whether we are happy and fulfilled or unhappy and disillusioned. *Happiness* is the by-product, not the goal, of a life dedicated to the search for our individual truth. That requires positive self-esteem as a base for the magnet of attraction that inevitably occurs throughout all time here. *Disillusionment* is what we can expect when we allow negative beliefs to infect our lives and draw bad things toward us. Each becomes a self-fulfilling prophecy. We must decide which one is for us.

And that's just it. The good news is that it *is* our choice. No one can give us what we need to be happy and no one can make us unhappy. Only we have the power to do that to ourselves.

Looking Beneath The Surface...

We find exactly what we're looking for.

Just as thoughts create our reality, our perceptions become our reality. We all see things through our own perceptual lenses, which is a combination of all the thoughts we have had to the moment. We are almost guilty of predisposing ourselves to certain attitudes based on how positive or negative our thinking patterns have been.

SEEK and you shall find means that what ever we look for, we *will* find. That is what projection is all about. We see in others the things we dislike about and recognize in ourselves. That's because we're not only looking for it, but we want to criticize it. When we criticize another, we criticize ourselves.

The only reason we are wild about something in another is because we are secretly accusing ourselves of the same offense. Beating yourself up at someone else's expense is a common human pastime.

Projection or Extension?

We will undoubtedly experience times in our lives when we dislike the behavior of someone who strangely acts (or we perceive them acting) much the same as we ourselves do. That's okay, because it's easier, at least on the surface, to criticize ourselves *through* other people. It might even be more convenient if it wasn't for the fact that we are simply postponing inevitable pain to ourselves and imposing it on someone else for the moment. It is not always so easy to 'see' our own faults, so we transfer them to someone else. This is why it is called PROJECTION.

An easy way to turn this around is to think of that person as one who is in need of extra care and consideration (like we are). This requires a change in our perception of the person (and ourselves). If we choose to EXTEND love and concern to that person instead of projecting anger and judgment, we may just experience inner peace and an increase in our own self-love. And why not? Just as in criticizing others, we criticize ourselves, through loving another we also learn to love ourselves.

The antithesis of projection then, is viewing a person's (offensive) behavior as a call for love ... to *extend* ourselves in service to that individual is about loving and accepting ourselves. It is one of our greatest gifts, and too often we forget that we were born with it ... the power to forgive and love unconditionally.

Since we will always have free will, we are at liberty to choose all the time. And when we err, to choose once again. We have another chance as we always get to begin again. Isn't it wonderful?

BOTTOM LINE in the search...or, WHAT NONE OF THE MATING BOOKS EVER TELLS YOU...

There IS NO one PERFECT! No one is "OUT THERE" waiting for you to "get there"...at least not physically, anyway.

How do we meet our perfect mate? The truth is there is really only one way. We need to *be* the person *we* were meant to be (that *is* perfect!) and the "right" person will get there -- and not a second sooner -- than he or she is supposed to.

We will recall my impression that there is still some mystical belief attached to the one perfect partner theory. Some consider how they may never find their magical person, others are certain that one wonderful day, this individual will walk straight into their lives, and everything will make sense. Either way, our thinking here is unfortunately backwards. It is backward because it is focused on the external, the other person, instead of ourselves.

What we need to understand is that there is no such person ... perfect in every way for us only, one sent from Heaven. This sounds like we are searching to find our "answer" in life; that we wish to fall in love with the one person who can meet our every need. We made this special person up, but he or she does not exist.

The reason that this is such a fairytale is because it is never about the other person, it is always and only about *us*. I am the one who must meet my own needs before I can hope to attract a meaningful someone into my life. This is mandatory and prerequisite. Whenever I look to the external world to meet my need, to make me happy, I will forever be disappointed. My true happiness and peace comes from within. I alone have that power. The "RIGHT" person comes once I have accomplished my personal happiness, because the attraction will be for the correct reasons.

A one-to-one match sounds mythical and magical and makes for good romance writing, but there is no Mr./Ms Right. There is more likely a *number* of individuals, each of whom could make a suitable partner... only we can't attract those folks if we're bent on a *one perfect person* mission ... or if we are busy attracting those who are matching up with our subconscious unfinished business. Although we generally settle on one partner, it doesn't mean that he or she was "the" one. When we believe in our own perfection, we draw unto ourselves people who fit, one of whom we choose.

Can We Ever Know Too Much?

It is said that ignorance is bliss, and while I will not go that far (knowledge is a good thing, to be sure), there is some merit to the "paralysis of analysis" argument. Here we are with the extremes, again. It should remain a red flag. What we do not want is to be foolish or "ignorant," but neither do we want to read into every conceivable gesture or word or lack thereof.

There is undoubtedly a glut of information out there with easy access. We do have amateur psychologists and are continually exposed to the psychobabble of the hour. What we need to be careful about is the illusion that someone else has the answer to your problem. Even erudite psychologists acknowledge that it is the patient who figures out their own problem. The professional is there to facilitate and draw out, but it is the individual who knows best and can most suitably identify what needs to be done to correct a problem in his or her own life.

The Biggest Secret About Falling In Love

If you haven't figured it out by now, the biggest secret about falling in love is that there really is no secret. But there is something most of us don't find out until we have made a few big blunders in the relationship department. That is, IT IS UP TO US individually. The only prerequisite to finding a love is being a love. Trying to love another without possessing self-love is a waste of everyone's time. It is impossible to give what we do not have. When we love ourselves unconditionally, we invite others to love us in the same way. It is the only way true love can happen.

That's it. That's why I wrote this whole book and that's why you read it. If you find that you are somewhat disappointed, it is likely that you haven't accepted responsibility yet. Don't worry, you will. It was never my intention to attempt to save you unnecessary hardship in making these discoveries on your own. I know that we can usually expect that each of us needs to learn in his own way, his own time. Perhaps it is not yet your time.

Still, I wish each of us all the love and warmth that this world has to offer, and for all of us to have someone's hand to hold through all the rough times and to share laughter with in all the good times. May we each love ourselves *into* the perfect relationship ... that is, the one we were intended to have.

♥ ♥ ♥

DateNotes

- Don't Look for anyONE to be your ANSWER because the answer is within you!
- You already possess all you need to be happy. The illusion is that someone makes you happy, the truth is that no one can.
- Be careful what you ask for because you are bound to get it. Remember that our subconscious works to make our beliefs come true because it doesn't know the difference between fantasy and reality.
- When it comes to love, we often confuse words or feeling with action. People can tell us that they "love" us and not act in loving ways toward us. While we may experience an intensity of feeling with another person, we need to understand that it will not always have to do with romantic love and long lasting relation ship.
- Instead of projecting our own guilt and wrongs onto someone else, why not try extending our love and understanding to liberate both of us from that judgement.
- Don't look for anything outside yourself to get you what you need.

- Your arrival in this world was controlled just as your exit from this world will be, so why not trust the middle of it to work just the way it is supposed to, without you trying so hard to control every outcome? Relax and trust; it's probably better than you could ever dream it would be without you in harsh command.

Epilogue

"LIVING WITH DETAILS"

Seldom, or perhaps never, does a marriage develop into an individual relationship smoothly and without crisis; there is no coming to consciousness without pain.

C.G. Jung,
Analytical Psychology, 1928

The book, and then subsequent movie version of *Bridges of Madison County* struck a cord with most women, especially those in "middle age" who felt they could identify with Francesca. This was a woman who had a yearning, as indefinable as it may have been to her on a conscious level, for a passionate connection to another human being. She hadn't disliked her life, in fact, she obviously loved her children and highly regarded the man she married. Yet somehow she came to view her life, in her words in the movie version, as "a life of details." We could feel her loneliness inside this family and we so wanted her to have more than she had. We felt Francesca's struggle too, when the opportunity of a lifetime presented itself and she was torn...between loyalty to her family and the passionate, unconditional love of a man with whom she could truly be alive.

We could have a number of different reactions to such a plot. We may have thought Francesca was right in her decision to remain with her family, after all, a commitment is a commitment, and it's not like her husband was a bad person or abusive, or unloving. And then we could have thought Francesca out of her mind not to have jettisoned her life of mediocrity in favor of romance and adventure. Perhaps she could have decided on some immoral compromise, remaining married but having a long-term affair with her lover.

The reason for the immense popularity and commercial success of such material is because there are far too many of us caught up in a dilemma of a life that asks 'what if.' We examine where we are with some sense that something is missing. We may have surrendered, believing that we had to marry the one we were with since we couldn't find the one that was meant only for us, the one "perfect" person, or just one more perfect than the one we have.

The reality is, "what ifs" are truly more enticing than what is, because they are unknown to us. Our imaginations can run wild and we can dream and believe in illusions. "If only" we had done this, or gone there, or said that, our lives may have been different. We could have--heck, we *should* have the life of our dreams.

Still, what we fail to consider oftentimes is that our time here is quite intentional. We are precisely where we need to be in order to accomplish what it is that we were intended to accomplish. The things that happen along the way for us are very purposeful, playing their own role in our meeting those intended objectives. Francesca's life was what it was supposed to be, and her meeting up with someone like Richard Kincaid was meaningful but it was not to be a lifetime relationship, at least not physically lifelong.

Perhaps the saddest part for us is not the realization that they could not be together but that this life has limitations and one of those limitations is that we can only love one partner at a time. Francesca no doubt had love for both her husband and Kincaid, but she could not have both--she had to make a decision. Perhaps we lament the choice of one at the expense of the other.

But that is the way it is. And one of the lessons may be that since life's many "details" include life-altering decisions, we will necessarily experience the pain which accompanies that. But the reward is clearly in having had the experience.

♥ ♥ ♥

All through this book I have hit on two themes, which may on the surface appear to be in conflict with one another. I repeatedly state how we should believe that once we become and love who we need to be, the "right" relationship will find its way to us. This seems to imply that we need to relax, take it easy, wait for it to happen. At the same time, there is information about marketing oneself in the dating arena and taking action in our search for a mate. In fact, these two concepts are not in conflict. We do need to believe that there will be a time when it is right for us. Believing this has a calming effect on us, as it quells our unnecessary fears and helps us focus on the positive. But believing also does not mean that we have to sit and wait.

Indeed it is our responsibility to pursue our happiness, and in that pursuit, it is incumbent upon us to take action in the direction of what we want. A positive belief, provides the guiding framework for us to remain open to experiences of dating and loving. It helps "ready" us to be able to develop the right relationship. And in that readiness, we allow and invite many potential partners from which we one day choose.

Alphabetical Reference List

Carnegie Dale;
How To Win Friends and Influence People

Cowan, Dr. Connell & Kinder, Dr. Melvyn;
Smart Women, Foolish Choices

DeAngelis, Barbara, Ph.D.;
How To Make Love All The Time

DeAngelis, Barbara, Ph.D.;
Are You The One For Me?

DeAngelis, Barbara, Ph.D.;
Secrets About Men Every Women Should Know

Fast, Julius;
The Incompatibility of Men and Women

Goleman, Daniel;
Emotional Intelligence

Gray, John, Ph.D.;
Men Are From Mars, Women Are From Venus

Hendrix, Harville, Ph.D.;
Keeping The Love You Find, A Guide For Singles

Hendrix, Harville, Ph.D.;
Getting The Love You Want, A Guide For Couples

Hillman, James;
The Soul's Code. In Search of Character and Calling

Jeffers, Susan, Ph.D.;
Opening Our Hearts To Men

Kreidman, Ellen;
Light His/Her Fire Tape Series

Kuriansky, Dr. Judy;
The Complete Idiot's Guide To Dating

Kushner, Harold S.;
How Good Do We Have to Be?

Mater, Rick, & Wing, Kathy;
Date To Win

Moore, Thomas;
SoulMates: Honoring the Mysteries of Love and Relationship

Nierenberg, Gerald I., and Calero, Henry;
How To Read A Person Like A Book

O'Connor, Dr. Margaret and Silverman, Dr. Jane;
Finding Love, Creative Strategies For Finding Your Ideal Mate

Peck, M. Scott, M.D.;
A World Waiting To Be Born

Penney, Alexandra;
How To Keep Your Man Monogamous

Powell, John, S.J.;
Why Am I Afraid To Tell You Who I Am?

Sills, Judith, Ph.D.;
A Fine Romance, The Psychology of Successful Courtship-Making It Will Work For You

♥♥♥

DATING AND THE PURSUIT OF HAPPINESS

This edition published 1998

by DRM NET INC.
5678 Main Street
Williamsville, New York 14221

ISBN: 0-966 308 9-0-5

1-800-217-1713
WWW.DATE-FINDER.COM
WWW.PLANETULTIMATE.COM